The
Heart of
Skye

Jim Crumley

Colin Baxter Photography, Grantown-on-Spey, Scotland

First Published in Great Britain in 1994 by
Colin Baxter Photography
Grantown-on-Spey
Morayshire, PH26 3NA
Scotland

British Library Cataloguing in Publication Data
Crumley, Jim
Heart of Skye
I. Title
914.118204

ISBN 0-948661-53-4

Printed in Great Britain

Front Cover Photograph © Colin Baxter 1994

The Heart of Skye

Love Durable as Gabbro

Walk with me, there is a shore
where love buoyantly drowns out
the ocean's dirge.

Sail with me, there is a tide
which love boards to blur
the horizon's distinctions.

Fly with me, there is an air
wherein love dances
among balletic eagles.

Climb with me, there is a mountain
where love durable as gabbro
weathers all storms.

To Val, Morag, Euan and Heather

Chapter One

Otter Dawn

I SEE IN my mind's eye as I write a heron on the end of a pier. It is fastened there by a full moon, and it peers down at a berthed boat like a derrick. That moon has just wakened me, boring in at a shoreline window, vast silver intruder. It says, 'come and see'. Temptress moon - you know me too well.

The Sound of Sleat is a silver wash from beneath the window sill to Beinn Sgritheall. Another inked-in heron shape scratches the wash with its flight and shrieks. The sound bounces off the water. It is 2.30am.

Listen. Search the night for its sounds. Catch a whiff of wind about the gable, the softest slap of water on shingle. Between heron shrieks there are curlew fragments, not the rich and drooling flight song of the spring moors but a soft-voiced Celtic snatch, like Uillean pipes. It begins again, a cry frail enough to shred on the edge of the wind. It is a fragment because it is night, it is winter and the bird is alone. Again, such a tantalising, elusive thing! I yearn for a longer movement of its rag-bag concerto, but the pitch alters abruptly to a short, shrill, three-syllable stab, nature's earliest morning alarm call. Perhaps there is an otter on the bird's shore. I cannot see the curlew, I cannot see the otter, if there is one to see. Just a heron on the end of the pier, stiff as a derrick.

How do you find the heart of an island? You begin by not looking for it at all, because when you begin, the idea does not exist. You do not even choose the island. You chance on it at a particularly susceptible moment in your life, you succumb to its aura, its landscape, its presence, its islandness, and you imbibe it all addictively for ever after. The island has chosen you. Perhaps you will eventually live there.

3.30am. I consult the window again. The window is open, the curtains parted and the flood of light has drowned all sleep's prospects. It takes ten minutes to dress in every layer of winter-thwarting clothing I can find and step softly through the door into the cold, monochrome blaze of the moonlight. It takes ten minutes more to accommodate the raw beauty. I tune into the night landscape before I move a yard from the door.

I have travelled to Skye addictively for twenty-five years, a hundred times by now, but I have not yet learned to live there. It could be that I never will. Skye's cause has not been greatly assisted by most of its incomers. Skye does not need me as much as I need Skye.

Isle Ornsay is snug under its sheltering hillside. The arms of its 'W'-shaped bay shut out all Skye and funnel your gaze past the island and its lighthouse to the Sound of Sleat, Beinn Sgritheall above the mouth of Loch Hourn, and the Knoydart peaks. The southmost shore of the bay is the suggestive curve which contains all that, suggestive, that is, of a pathway towards the deeper intimacies of the landscape beyond the funnel. Now it is a black swirl, beckoning as persuasively as the moon at the window or a voice in a dream.

So I have acknowledged the addiction, but still, I had been through twenty of its twenty-five years before the heart of an island crept up on me, another two or three at least before I thought about trying to pin it down. But how? And where to look? And what to look for? And anyway, why so long?

Ten feet away, a curlew stands on a rock, one-footed, bathed in moonlight, head towards tail, dipping curve of bill laid in dipping curve of spine. An eye blinks open and the speck of the moon glims whitely there. It registers nothing in my dark and still silhouette, blinks closed again, shutting down its tiny moon gleam. I pass by, pause, look back. Now the bird is all silhouette and with none of its characteristic head-and-sabre curlew shape it might just as well be a rock, a rock which wakes from time to time with the moon in its eye and plays the Uillean pipes like an angel.

Far across the bay, a squabble of oystercatchers takes wing, briefly piercing and percussive, no angel-pipers these. When the bickering stops the silence deepens. I try to step more quietly, suddenly conscious that of all the moving creatures of the darkness I am the only one which moves a small stone when it walks.

Why so long? is the easy question to answer. Having had an island choose me, and having suffered all the highs and lows of addiction as it evolved, I had to learn to love Skye, an apprenticeship of appreciation. Skye is fifty miles from stem to stern, and there are many hundreds of miles in its crooked coasts. There remain places I have never been and there are a few I hardly ever miss, like Isle Ornsay. Now there is a certain fond familiarity with landmarks large and small, in a handful of cases even with individual birds and beasts; among the islanders there are a few friends. All that took twenty years of purposeful and purposeless exploration among those parts of Skye which I almost never miss, so that I began to feel confident in their midst, not a belonging (for that is the prerogative of the Skye people and a very, very few incomers who have taken great pains to adopt the Skye yoke) but a sense of empathetic participation. I have come to learn, too, the dread of leaving Skye again, the feared withdrawal which is the price of all addiction. That is the answer to the question, 'Why so long?' The imperfect and incomplete answers to the other questions are the basis of what follows.

The mainland mountains advance and magnify in the moonlight. Beinn Sgritheall, dowsed in snow, shows its best profile from here, a mountain so familiar in my life I am inclined to greet it as a close friend. From the headland at the mouth of the bay I consider its snow cap. What colour? White? Yellow? Blue? Silver? Gray? I am convinced by none of them and give up.

Eyes and ears attune to a new pitch of attentiveness in my surroundings. Stillness becomes easier. The headland begins to fit in its brilliant darkness like a black hand in a black glove. I have detected a new pattern on the water, twenty yards offshore. At the head of it is the blunt thrust of an otter muzzle from which a vee-shaped wake spills quietly, its edges and ripples defined by glints of moonlight. The otter's presence comes as no surprise, merely a delight, for this is a classic otter shore. There is one beast with a holt not far from here which I have watched many times, a big dog otter, thick-necked, dark-crowned, but with a dull ginger 'muffler' about neck and jowls tempering his sleek profile with a clown's face. It is a reasonable cosmetic conclusion: any adult otter is a lethal and lovable cocktail of missile and clown. Whether or not this is the same beast, I have no way of knowing, but there is a tremulous and throat-tightening thrill crouching alone on that dark headland watching an otter swim obliviously through this kingdom of otters, through the otter's night world. For a few moments in which he crosses the small bay beyond the headland, passes the headland and swims on across the mouth of Isle Ornsay's bay, I am as natural a part of this world as he is and he has paid me no more attention than he has accorded the roosting curlew. This is the kind of situation my instincts feed off.

Those instincts now say: you have reached the wildest corner of the shore in the dark and without troubling the bay's wildlife, so sit, become a rock, be in a rock's guise when daylight dawns and have nature treat you accordingly. See what happens.

The instincts say nothing about the zero temperature, nothing about the two hours or so between now and dawn. The instincts say sit. I sit.

The otter is back in twenty minutes, porpoising further out, more or less retracing his route, detectable more by the pattern of disturbance on the water, the moonlit ripples, than by any discernible otter shape. For a few yards of his journey the long blunt 'floating log' shape materialises as he passes my headland then fades, but as I strain to follow the front of the wake it begins to curve abruptly back towards me. Its progress, to my ears at least, is silent. It ripples closer.

The otter dives, his tail is the last to go under with a pronounced slap, he resurfaces to climb sea-sleekit from the water onto a flat rib of rock five yards away.

The moon turns him pale, but it is a pale imitation of the moonlight that was, for the orb has put down behind the mountains and only a lightening of the darkness betrays what has been. Still, there is enough to pale a dripping otter, and now he stands and stares at my rock shape (as I fancy it). Did he detect me from the water? If he did, it was not by scent, not with an onshore wind. Is he so fluent in the topography of the shore that one new dark rock shape in a shoreline of dark rock shapes is recognisable as alien and must be investigated? Curiosity is the badge of the weasel tribe and the otter is of that tribe. He is curious.

I command every nerve I own to stillness. He is a yard further up the rock now, so close that I don't even need the failed moonlight to see every detail of his face, every glistening whisker. My face is hooded and he won't be seeing much of it, but from where he stands, I do not smell like a rock.

Without warning, he loses interest. He turns, stops at the water's edge, looks back, scratches an ear, steps into the sea and is gone under a thin cluster of travelling bubbles.

In the next hour I hear this: three times the call of a tawny owl down the coast, twice the sudden tremolo of curlew, twice a brief stridency of oystercatchers, once a heron rasp (and its slow sea-level flight ghosts past me to alight on a rock twenty yards away where it stands like an unlit standard lamp), once a far-off shrill scream which may or may not have been one of Sandaig's badgers. The slap and suck of the Sound's waters underscore all that, filling rhythmically the long silences.

You become in such circumstances a little less human, a little more of nature, but only a little. The thrilling unease at your surroundings to which you accustom only slowly – that is not a thing of nature. The slow infiltration of cold which eventually overwhelms your bones and soaks intravenously into every nerve-end in your body – that reveals poorer tolerances than nature. You shiver, then you shiver uncontrollably, and there is the urge to counter that with movement, but you are supposed to be a rock. The one characteristic of rock you must respect (and the only one you can emulate) is immobility. The cold settles to a dull ache, the shivering stops, you sit on and on. You know that nature will contrive something to rescue you eventually. The one thought you must shut out is that you can get up any time you like and walk away from it, back to the warmth of your bed. To do that would be to fall back on the one option which is not open to nature. At 4am on a midwinter morning, nature is cold. Besides, you have done the hard part – hasn't instinct already told you so? You can now revel in the luxury of merely being still. You know that soon nature will turn something up, even if it is only daylight. You wash your mind clear again. You sit on and on.

Sky and water pale, land blackens. Detail emerges close at hand. A dark rock by your left foot reveals itself as a red rock, a small and utterly unexpected transformation. Lighthouses materialise beneath their lights. You hear a car, a crow, a boat, a called greeting back in the township. The distant sounds reach you like details of a dream through a sleep of cold. Bird shapes are flying. Curlew and oystercatcher rev up and start to call, almost constantly now. Gulls mobilise and wail and mew and screech. A blackbird begins to sing – no warm-up, just instant and full-throated song for five unbroken minutes, an illusion of spring which finally disintegrates into alarm. There is a cat beneath his singing perch. It is almost light. The otter is back, twenty-five yards offshore. Nature has turned something up.

The otter is on his back, eating an eel which writhes in his 'hands' as it dies a few inches at a time. It does not do to dwell on how that feels to the eel. The otter dives, resurfaces with a crab clamped in the widest gape of his jaws. He cannot deal with the crab as he deals with an eel. He needs a shoreline rock and he chooses mine, the same one he chose last time. He swims towards me, crab first. One pincer flails out of the water. Otters like their meat fresh.

He climbs onto the rock, drops the crab, looks round. I hear the crab fall. His teeth take hold and I hear the shell crack and splinter and I hear his teeth crunch and grind. Flakes of crab fall into the water, a brittle rain. Then he discovers me, not ten yards away. He turns for the water but his mind is torn. It is a big crab. He turns again, and like the big weasel he is, stands two-footed. He pronounces an interrogation:

'Haaaahhhh?'

I copy the sound: 'Haaaahhhh!'

He is puzzled: 'Haaaahhhh?'

'Haaaahhhh!'

He drops to all fours, takes a pace up the rock:

'Haahh!' More authoritative now. This rock which answers him back but does not smell like a rock or even look much like one but does not behave much like a creature either is clearly unadventurous, timid, unworthy of further attention. He turns his back on me. The crab flakes fall again. Occasionally he glances back over one shoulder. After ten minutes there are only scraps of shell on the rock; wind and tide will account for them soon enough. He steps off, makes no sound, and is gone in his bubble-cloud. Suddenly I remember the heron standard lamp, but somewhere in the past two hours it rose and left with such discretion that I missed it.

The sun touches the summit snows of Beinn Sgritheall. It is 9am. Standing is a curious and reassuring sensation, walking a stiff and painful one as the blood begins to rediscover its old haunts in my legs. Breakfast is long and slow and unreal. Reality was the otter dawn and a glimpse of the beginning of nature's day, the beginning of everything.

How do you find the heart of an island? You could do worse than begin by searching between two herons, one that looks like a derrick, one like a standard lamp.

Chapter Two

The Beginning of Everything

SKYE IS AN eagle or a butterfly. If you hold to the theory that the very name is from the Gaelic An t-Eilean Sgitheanach, the Winged Isle, the shape of Skye supports the idea well enough. The eagle option thrusts its wings high in a predatory strike, its wing tips at Duntulm and Waternish Head, its head bearing down in Kyleakin and Kylerhea, its talons slung loosely below at Point of Sleat. Here is the 'golden glimmer of the Skye bird' in Sorley MacLean's phrase.

The butterfly faces north-east, and is about to alight on Raasay. Flodigarry and Kyleakin are the leading edges of its forewings, the Point of Sleat and Neist Point the trailing edges of its rear wings. Whether eagle or butterfly, the Cuillin form the unquestionable body of the creature, a hub around which the whole Skye landscape whirls in a chaotic slaister of wings and wild winds. It is an old image, that of Skye as a Winged Isle, never better invoked than by that clearest Island voice which is the Gaelic poetry of Sorley MacLean. This is from his own translation of his poem, *An t-Eilean* – 'The Island':

> I fancied
> the great ocean itself restless
> agitated with love of you

as you lay on the sea,
great beautiful bird of Scotland,
your supremely beautiful wings bent
about many-nooked Loch Bracadale,
your beautiful wings prostrate on the sea
from the Wild Stallion to the Aird of Sleat,
your joyous wings spread
about Loch Snizort and the world . . .

The title of Sorley MacLean's poem permits me one small explanation, for now I have spelled the word 'Island' with a capital 'I'. It is because the Island is the Islanders' other name for Skye. They may live on only one of Scotland's hundreds of offshore islands, but all others are mere islands, or so it seems from Skye. Skye, *the* Island, is their superior in every way. It is a judgement I have not been able to fault. Yet such is the size and scope of Skye that it often cloaks its Islandness in distance. The landscapes of Sleat and Trotternish, for example, might belong to different worlds. Trotternish's collapsing shelves and trembling rock pillars and hacked crags have been used by film makers to convey the landscape of some lost planet, and for all their familiarity to me, they still looked convincing enough in their other-worldly film star role. The trick, I suppose was to keep the Cal-Mac steamers out of shot. But if you journey from Sleat to Staffin without stopping, you have the feeling of travelling to a different part of Scotland, rather than a different part of Skye, so complete is the transformation. Skye, the Island, the great beautiful bird, the vulnerable butterfly, is a complex beast.

I fear for that bird-butterfly now that it has been manacled to mainland Scotland by its embryonic road bridge. What I fear is that the sense of Skye's Island nature will suffer irreparably. It is not the kind of argument which impresses developers, governments or public inquiries, but it goes deep with a lot of Islanders. It is as difficult to explain as it is to deny that in many people on Skye it is a real fear.

But writers from furth of Skye are forever pronouncing on the place and the best that I can say of the company I keep when I so pronounce is that some of it is distinguished and some of it pedestrian. We have in common that we haunt the Island for images, and that we stand in a tradition of response to nature and landscape which is as old as man, and if I go beyond writers and align myself with such as Mendelssohn and Turner too, it is only for the sake of the argument. We are, or were, all trying to pin down our own idea of a landscape which happens to be where someone else lives. In my own case, I can argue with fierce conviction that the Skye landscape also happens to live in me regardless of where my characteristic restlessness happens to hang its hat.

T Ratcliffe Barnett was a writer somewhere between distinguished and pedestrian (like most of us), a bit keen on a bogus strain of romanticism, but a man who tramped the ground often and knew well his own definition of the Island. In his 1946 book, *Autumns in Skye, Ross and Sutherland*, he wrote:

'From Ardvasar it is an up-and-down road all the way to the Aird of Sleat . . . I have lit my fire on that glamorous road that leads to the end of everything.' But all that ends at Aird of Sleat is tarmac, beyond which a species of road-cum-track lurches west to the ocean and degenerates south to the lighthouse at Point of Sleat. It is there, specifically, where I have stood uncounted times, knee-deep in my own symbolism and with all Skye before me and all the delectable bird-butterfly wing of Sleat for my day's wandering that I have found the beginning of everything.

I like the company of lighthouses. They are, by definition, uncompromising, out-on-a-limb places, landfall of ocean storms and storm-hurled birds, the acceptable imprint of man on the kind of landscapes where you would find the presence of any other building an affront. Many of Skye's wing tips and lesser headlands have their beacons. I warm to them not just because of where they are, but also because of an old childhood association which belongs on the other side of the country.

One of the redeeming features of the flat in Dundee where I spent my teenage years was a view which encompassed a vast swathe of the Tay estuary. On the clearest of days, a tiny white smudge on the eastmost horizon was the Bell Rock lighthouse, something like twenty-five miles away, perched alone on a solitary rock which has its foundations deep in the bed of the North Sea. On the clearest nights its light was unmistakable. For me it was symbolic of wilder worlds, an almost incomprehensible solitude then which I have since learned to comprehend, and occasionally to welcome. I invested that light on its rock with journeyers, uncanny vessels, and seagoing birds. I thought of it as friend to those whales and other deep sea pilgrims which ply that thoroughfare of all Europe. In my imagination, and in the skyline presence of that far light, I acquired a taste for islands long before I ever set foot on one.

Then there were days and nights when the horizon was unseen, masked by a gray blur, and I would paint in my mind the view from the unseen rock itself. To be there now, I would think, what does it feel like? No sight or sound of land through 360 degrees beyond that one small and stubborn stump of underwater rock and the thump and thunder of the sea, the wail of wind and bird for conversation, sporadic whales for passers-by. Years later, the nearest I ever came to knowing how it might feel, I stood on the summit of Connachair on St Kilda and felt an inkling of kinship with the old keepers of the Bell Rock light. But even on St Kilda, you can always go for a walk.

So when I turn left at the ocean coast beyond the Aird of Sleat and wander the track to the lighthouse on Sleat's wing tip, I journey not just to the beginning of Skye, but also to the beginning of everything which ever helped to shape my love of islands, and my love of *the* Island in particular.

Sleat at sunset. It is almost a cliche of Skye, the sun putting down behind the Cuillin or toppling off the edge of one of that small gaggle of lesser islands anchored off Skye. In my mind as I write is a straggle of hours which commemorate the cliche as compulsive theatre-in-landscape. The sun crossed low over Canna, paused on the very brim of Soay then fell off, so forge-red that I half expected the sea to steam.

How to write down such a sunset? It has been tried so often with so many conspicuous and famous failures. Gavin Maxwell tried often and failed to convince, an astonishing lapse in one of so many literary gifts. Seton Gordon was another – he was better at sunrises. You need, perhaps, the comparable skills of Turner. He would have been quite unafraid of it, wading into his sea without pause, fastening the sun to the centre of the canvas, brilliantly breaking the rules. He never shirked a challenge to match nature's sense of outrage against his own. His watercolour of Coruisk, which is on show every January in the National Gallery of Scotland in Edinburgh, and the tumultuous oil which followed (and is now in the Tate's permanent Turner exhibition in London) take as many liberties with the painting of the subject as nature did when that masterpiece among island landscapes was sculpted in the first place.

Even allowing for the obvious differences, I am no Turner. But I share his love of the outrage in nature, and confronted by centre-stage sun and the operatic tremendousness of its island-and-mountain stage set, I searched for something with which to pin my sunset to the centre of its canvas. I found a pair of cormorants.

They emerged into my sightline from some secretive shadow of Bla Bheinn where its black south ridge laddered up to its high and hellish heaven. As they flew, they slit the sun's water ribbon as one. For a moment their cloak of feathers and skin was shed and the raw and blood-red birds flew on.

They were cormorant-black again at once; the sun dived into the deeps so signalling the beginning of an endless dusk, the like of which I can never expect to see again. But with Skye, who knows?

The dusk worked for its effect in ever paler shades among the ever darkening fragments of land – Rum and its small island acolytes, Soay pancaked on a flame-shaded ocean, the prow of Gars-bheinn (cutting edge of the Cuillin) and all its blue-black gabbro cronies. I thought of Loch Coruisk, that mountain heart where unseen in blue shadow, its waters paled. I was motionless for long hours, moved by the incomprehensible forces of nature. To this day I paint all my cormorants on all my western shores in scarlet.

I had resolved that in the writing of this book I would not let the Cuillin overwhelm it the way they overwhelm the Skye visitor. I would stow them away in their own chapter and leave it at that, but the Cuillin would have none of it, and I find myself dwelling on them already from Sleat before the book has taken one serious northward step on its journey through the Island. For the reality of Skye is that the Cuillin are forever butting in on your thoughts, catching your eye on the skyline when you least expect them, blue or black or gray or white or brown, or host to the one cloud in a cloudless watercolour wash of sky, a far nagging presence or a comforting one, a signature of the Island scribbled in gabbro hieroglyphics. Or if you are in Elgol or Drynoch or Carbost or Portnalong, they exert outrageous influence. In such proximity, there have been times when I have felt uncomfortable turning my back on them.

The only places to avoid them (strictly on an out-of-sight-is-out-of-mind basis) are hunkered down on Sleat's east coast or locked in behind the rock bars of the Prison high on Trotternish's spine. Even with such landscape bulwarks at your back, the temptation to go furtively up over Sleat's watershed to Tarskavaig or Ord, or sclim through the Prison roof on to Meall na Suiramach is almost a compulsion – just to see them again, just to know they are there, just to put them in their place in the landscape's scheme of things.

So from the singular lighthouse at Point of Sleat, I looked across that small outcrop of the Atlantic which splinters into Loch Eishort and Loch Slapin on one side of Strathaird and Loch Scavaig on the other, looked past Eilean na h-Airde which is Strathaird's southmost outpost, past Beinn Bhreac on Soay which rides at anchor under the harbouring blue-gray girth of the Cuillin. At this, their most impressive distance, I can restore to the Cuillin all their legendary might, all their landscape glories over which my own generation of Skye travellers has ridden roughshod, wounding the mountains.

I have a problem with the Cuillin, or rather with what they have become. Dawa Tenzing, the Sherpa who climbed into mountaineering and human immortality alongside Edmund Hillary on Everest, confessed many years later that he had climbed fearfully, craving the mountain's forgiveness for every step he cut in its side. There was nothing made of this at the time, and the western world cared little for the idea of conservation then, although it had been a deeply ingrained component of the Sherpa psyche for centuries. Tenzing would articulate in time the placid outrage he and his countrymen felt and still feel at the assault on what to them is a sacred landscape:

'The foreigners see the mountains. We see only ourselves. We *are* the mountains. The mountains are the bone. We are the blood.'

Without making Himalayan claims for the Cuillin, or a Sherpa-like landscape-reverence for the Gael, it is a view for which I have much sympathy. It is no longer possible – as it once was, even within my own lifetime – to feel in the Cuillin the bone of the

Island, a kinship in the same Island body. The Cuillin today, as in Tenzing's Himalaya (where twenty or thirty people on the summit of Everest in one day has become unexceptional), are polluted by too many people being seen and not seeing, being heard and not hearing, and worst of all, not feeling.

I have no Himalayan mountain gods to cling to, but if there is a Scottish mountain landscape worthy of finer feelings in those who cross its path, it is surely that of the Skye Cuillin. My own response to what has befallen the Cuillin is not to climb. Instead I hold the mountains at arms' length from such as the Point of Sleat or Elgol or Soay, according them the respect of distance, and from that distance to try and rediscover a sense of being blood to the mountains' bone. I set as much store by them as that, and would rather hold them impregnably out of reach forever.

It is enough now to be in their shadow, or to walk quietly and alone, forsaking the incomparable ridges, and crossing in a November mist to Coruisk by way of pilgrimage. In my mind whenever I think of the ridges now is a day of ten years ago when I crossed to Glen Brittle in May and found Blackpool under canvas. The sight recalled with some revulsion a Japanese expedition on Mount Everest which was mounted so that one man could attempt to ski down it. The lingering image of its shallow motive was of support climbers at base camp watching portable televisions, re-runs of 'Bonanza' with dubbed Japanese dialogue. I turned my back on the Glen Brittle day and walked alone over the low summits of Sleat, from Sgiath-bheinn Chrossavaig to Sgurr na h-Iolaire to Sgurr nan Caorach, and every time I lifted my eyes across Tarskavaig Bay I would set the Cuillin at their preferred untouchable distance. Given the opportunity now, it is not a national park I would throw round the Cuillin with its inevitable management policies of 'come-hither' bureaucracy, but a cordon of sanctity. Too much has already gone to be able to rely on compromise, and wounded gabbro is slow to heal. It is only by leaving the Cuillin alone to the exclusive company of nature that healing can begin. The American naturalist Aldo Leopold wrote in a matchless book, *A Sand Country Almanac*, 'All conservation of wildness is self-defeating, for to cherish we must see and fondle, and when enough have seen and fondled, there is no wilderness left to cherish.'

So I preach my small gospel of the benevolence of distance, but it is noticeable that I am usually alone when I preach it. Leopold also wrote: 'We abuse land because we regard it as a commodity which belongs to us. When we regard it as a community to which we belong, we may start to use it with love and respect.' My own gospel says amen to that, but the gulf between the ideologies of commodity and community in today's Cuillin is depressingly wide and grows wider.

Chapter Three

A Moment Among Eagles

SLEAT is a good place to watch eagles, but none of my hours watching them was quite as remarkable as a late winter afternoon driving back to Isle Ornsay and believing my day's work was done.

As I left Tarskavaig I slipped a cassette into the car stereo and ambled round the bay into that tight and twisty gorge which hoists up among the fractured moors giddy with hill burns, freckled with lochans. The music was the guitarist John Williams playing Rodrigo's *Fantasia Para Un Gentilhombre*, the first movement of which ended as I emerged from the trees of the gorge into one of those moments of an almost divine timelessness which seem to punctuate my nature writer's life at long intervals. It is certainly the only one I can think of which happened on four wheels – in fact it depended on the car for its effect. At the precise moment of that brief silence between the end of the first movement and the beginning of the second, an eagle slid low over the crest of Sithean Mor drifting more or less east below the skyline. The bird slowed, dipped and lowered to a few feet above the hill face, and flying at a breath above stalling speed, began to hunt the ground, slow as a harrier, at which point the music resumed.

I had hardly been listening until then, but at the first notes of the adagio, a slow stalking low-register guitar theme, I had an extraordinary sense of orchestrating the eagle flight, so sweetly did bird and guitar dovetail. It was as if the best of our wildlife cameramen, say Hugh Miles, had plotted the perfect Skye collaboration with a film composer of equal standing, John Barry perhaps. Now a daring director was at work, for the eagle began to travel the hillside at the same slow-motion pace, a single wing beat sustaining the headway at intervals of about fifty yards, parallel to the road and perhaps fifty feet above it while the music spun out its own inexorable thread of golden brown. I had stopped the car by now and wound down the window, craning to follow the flight, and I felt the first splashes of a fast and light ocean shower spatter my face. The raindrops felt as I had never felt rain before, sharp and soft at once, a kindly sting, and became strands of a web of heightened sensations in which I had become enmeshed.

The bird flew on, still following the line of the hill and the hill road, and I had a bizarre idea that I could 'stalk' him in the car. I set off on the most enthralling and unlikely mile I have ever driven although the speed rarely rose above 15 miles an hour and I diced several times with the rocky and ditched roadside with my eyes locked on the eagle. At every dip or bend or brief blindness in the road I was sure I would emerge beyond it to find the eagle had disappeared, but each time I found the bird again at once holding its course and its altitude. I fell in behind it again on the empty road while the music mimicked the bird's fluidity, a harmony beyond the scope of mere listening. The eagle itself had entered into the spirit of the composer's adagio, or at least so I fancied from my unique position. But the music changed the mood itself, for the composer interrupts the adagio's flow by first a fanfare and then a dance, and it was at this point that I improvised a new ploy in what had already become a quite surreal episode. I would overtake the eagle. I would park beyond the summit of the road and I would photograph the eagle as it flew past.

So with fanfares and twosteps dinning in my ears I hurtled a bend or two, crossed the summit, parked, grabbed the camera and waited for the eagle to reappear while the music slipped back into the reprise of the adagio's theme. The whole thing was a preposterous idea. I was vaguely aware of a kind of suppressed arrogance which now presumed to orchestrate nature, and the flight of an eagle of all unorchestrateable things, but I suspect, too, something of the old hunter's instinct was at work. Although I had travelled on wheels rather than on foot, although I had made no attempt at concealment, and although my 'quarry' was a concocted mental image rather than a beast I might slay, I had made what I could of the prevailing conditions and now lay in wait, adrenalin pumping, heart thumping, to catch – what?

Reconsidering the moment now a couple of years after the event, it was more than a fusion of flight and music and photographic image I was after. I was Turner, pinning my blood-red sun to the centre of the canvas, ensnaring the focal point of memory so that it would stay pin-sharp and vivid, so that it would sustain me until I tire of Skye and eagles which is not likely to happen in this lifetime.

The eagle completed the sequence perfectly on cue, for the music had now resumed the eagle-flight adagio theme as the bird reappeared. Then as it drew level with the car it snapped the spell with a powerful swerving climb up the hillside. In three immense wing beats the eagle had lifted above the skyline where the sun burnished the gold necklace of the bird, then in three more beats the eagle was over the hill crest, gone.

I said 'Cut!' aloud to myself, switched off the music, and in the Skye quiet, caught a glimpse of my own wide smile in the car's door mirror. Any habitual wanderer of the wilds will know such moments which follow the witnessing of nature's most captivating gestures: it is as if you have stepped beyond yourself and from a discreet distance you gaze on your own face flushed with the delight and the joy and the privilege of what you have seen and felt. There is no-one there to share it with (and often such things are beyond communication anyway) so you share it with yourself. They are the golden hours, and they are what it is all about.

Each time I cross that road now, I drive with an eye on the skyline, for it will always be a good piece of eagle terrain, but I never had the nerve to play the Rodrigo again. You cannot recreate such things any more than you can anticipate them. The best you can hope for is that once or twice in a lifetime the blessed fluke of circumstance crosses your path, and that your soul is sensitive enough to tune in when it does. If you are lucky, you can reassemble the moment at the drop of an eagle wing, at the sound of the first few guitar notes, at the rediscovery amid a small chaos of slide boxes of what turned out to be an indifferent picture of an eagle silhouette, or every time you point your car up through that tight and twisty gorge which hoists up among the fractured moors giddy with hill burns, freckled with lochans.

Chapter Four

The Melancholy Garden

IT IS SAID of Sleat that it is the Garden of Skye. It is a myth, the work of the tourist industry. The myth relies for the substance of its illusion on the fact that if you define Sleat (as many travellers do) as the ribbon of road from the ferry at Armadale to Loch na Dal you are spared the rasp of the ocean wind and your way is shaded with illusory trees. There are lush, brambly places along the shore and the planted gardens of Armadale Castle both heighten and deepen the illusion.

Reality is that the castle gardens, however impressive, have nothing to do with the true beauties of Skye. Rather they are the one tolerable legacy of that unhappy era when clan chieftains all across Gaelic Scotland were flattered and bought into submission by London whilst their people were crudely cleared and broken. Armadale's gardens are the early 19th century's monument to the Macdonald chieftains' squalid delusions of grandeur. They are arguably beautiful, but it is not something to celebrate that Sleat has such a garden.

Besides, the Garden of Skye is perhaps one per cent 'garden' and ninety-nine per cent rock and bog and moor and lochan and cliff. Where native trees survive they are scraps and remnants of the woodland that once was, thrawn survivors through oppressive centuries of felling and overgrazing by sheep. The Garden of Skye is not half the garden it once was.

There *are* trees at Dalavil, and there is bracken and bog, there is a faltering footpath and there is the green stain and the smattering of stones and shapes on the ground which were once homes. The people who lived at Dalavil were as indigenous as the trees, as much a product of the nature of the place. The trees have taken a little longer to die out here than the people, but only because they have been treated with careless neglect rather than brutally cleared. Dalavil is wild now, but its wild beauties are overlayed by a profound melancholy, a well where too much drinking is dangerous. I have been there twice and I am not at all sure that I will go back.

Dalavil lies at the west end of one of a handful of glens which cross the Sleat peninsula. The others have good single track roads, but Gleann Meadhonach's lack of a road was the excuse to clear Dalavil in the 1870s . . . and any excuse was excuse enough then. The Education Act insisted on a school, the estate decided that was too expensive and it was cheaper to uproot the crofters. So they left with no say in the matter and Dalavil has withered and wildered ever since. The history of the Highland Clearances is stiff with such excuses, the motive always the same: the maximum profit and the minimum inconvenience for an accursed breed of morally corrupt landlords. The melancholy you now sense is the legacy of the cleared families. Writer David Craig commemorates them in a compassionate and vigorous book, *On the Crofter's Trail*:

> Here in Dalavil the people had prayed and sung psalms to the sound of running water. Children as they grew older looked up at the terraced backdrop of Doire na h-Achlais where wild water sheds its veils and jets of spume and wondered, "When will it stop? Why does it come in jerks instead of smoothly?" And thought this over and over

again as their senses curled out to understand the world. The mothers and fathers loved and hated each other, the conditions allowed of no daily escape, to the pub or down the motorway – although the men (and the single women) could escape for seasons at a time if need or fancy drove them as guest-workers to the mainland, where they lifted potatoes in the big fields of Ayrshire and Angus or brought in hefty harvests with their own sickles that they had carried with them over the kyle and over the mountains.

You could say that here humanity tried to establish itself and failed, over a period small in the eye of time but long in the minds of the tyauving families. The final families at Dalavil did not fail, they were terminated (with extreme prejudice to use a CIA term). And the lack of a school was only an excuse. The estate and the incoming farmers wanted the best land, the broad well-grassed glen bottoms, for the wintering of their sheep and they wanted the hill land – the crofters' traditional grazings – for summer pasture and later for sport.

The sheep still graze the glen bottom and the summer hills and gather by a ruin on the shore of Loch a' Ghlinne to shelter from the sea wind with which all life in Gleann Meadhonach must come to terms. The wood, which is still called Coille Dalavil, is dying on its feet for the want of a fence or someone who cares about its fate. Pine, birch, oak, ash, they dance laboriously to the wind's tune, and the sheep and the few deer account for every young tree. Perhaps another hundred years and the woods of Dalavil will also have been terminated, with extreme prejudice.

I first saw Dalavil on a showpiece day for all the world's autumns. It was as if that season had heaped all its best eggs into one basket then spilled them across my path as I drove south from

Isle Ornsay. Beinn Sgritheall and the other peaks across the Sound had hauled down the year's first snow in the night, not a big fall, just a capping of the top five hundred feet, just enough to make them look Himalayan. By 9am the sun was warming to its task of vanquishing the forces of the snow-bringer. Dalavil's birches and brackens wore all gold's shades and a sea breeze set them jigging with a festive and infectious fervour. The loch barely stirred, blue milk, and I watched an eagle climb above it in a spiral which took the bird quite beyond my vision, with or without binoculars.

I spent the whole day at Dalavil, followed its river to the sea, explored its woods, sprang along its ridges, my eyes swithering between the charms of low-profile Sleat and the headier charms of the Cuillin and Rum. I was infected by that same buoyancy which seemed to have gripped nature. In the early evening I was by the loch again, brewing coffee and sensing the pervasive sadness which attends all still hours in such places when I heard above the hiss of the stove and the soft slap of the loch the sound that I love best in all nature, the muted brass notes of whooper swans in flight. Seven came low upriver, crossed the loch shore and glided down to land. The stillness of the water was deepening in the fading light and at the east end of the loch the water looked quite white. It was there the swans landed and in the instant before they did so, as they crossed the white water, they were suddenly darker than their background, suddenly not white but a purplish gray. At the same moment their reflection rose to meet them in the water, the same dark shade, and the swans' numbers doubled instantly and briefly to fourteen. The birds settled on the water calling loudly, their cries skidding over the water and the glen and echoing back from the ridges in a wondrous chaos of sounds and half sounds. I wondered how familiar the glen's old inhabitants must have been with the sound, and whether they ever grew weary of it, or whether they only wearied of its absence when the birds wheeled north in April.

I walked out that evening with an autumn moon to light my path and the rasp of Sleat's handful of stags haranguing each other and their counterparts across the Sound. I wondered if that confusion of tides and shores and hillsides and echoes ever baffled them, tantalised them with imaginary rivals which were nothing more that the echo of a mainland beast catching a stray wind, bouncing off a rock or the vagaries of tidal eddy, so that a Sleat stag would round on the sound, roaring, confronting nothing. Or were they always too tuned in to nature's sleight of hand to be fooled? I did not forget Dalavil.

There was a second visit. Three days before it I was staying with friends near Plockton and gave them a copy of my book, *A High and Lonely Place*. The book's dust jacket carries the sub-title 'The Sanctuary and Plight of the Cairngorms' which prompted my host to comment: 'Isn't it so sad that the sanctuary *and* the plight are everywhere now,' and because I was on a weekend break from a protracted stay on Skye at the time, he added, 'the sanctuary and the plight of Skye, for example.' I nodded my agreement, and as we roamed around the plight of Skye's many sanctuaries, I remembered Dalavil again, spoke of its old plight, of the sanctuary it had since become for swans and solace seekers like me. I knew I would be back three days later.

I remembered the rough and fragmentary track down the brackeny hillside below the road to Auchnacloich. A flat gray sky bore down on the day and the Island, darkening my mood. A sluggish sea wind beat west across Sleat in gusts. A golden eagle looking more black than golden against such an unflattering sky came low over my hillside, close enough for me to see the white wing and tail patches of its immaturity, and at my sudden appearance she drove hard for a moorland edge and landed beside a second bird. There they sat while I dropped into the glen, and each time I turned to look back, I could see their heads and craning necks above the heather like two preposterously overgrown grouse. I watched them until my eyes ached in the glasses and my head and arms and hands hurt with the effort of holding the glasses steady in the fluctuating wind, but the birds barely moved. They appeared to have lapsed into that state of torpor which settles on many large birds of prey for hours at a time, and which compels them to do nothing. The birds are not unalert, for that would go against nature's grain, but they seem eager for inactivity. They are not spying the land or watching for prey or the return of a mate or a parent. They are simply being. Time is passing and they want no part of it.

I stiffened beyond the point of mere discomfort and moved off with a wave to them, leaving them to their being. The winter glen on such a day is a drab place until you crest a small rise in the ground, a matter of a few feet, and see the loch and its woods and its small ruin half a mile ahead and the sudden prospect lifts the whole enterprise. It was then that I saw the road, newly carved into the flank of the glen, a bulldozed mile-long snake from the Auchnacloich road down to the Dalavil woods and the loch shore. The crudest road-building techniques had been used, lacerations on the face of the land. The object of the exercise is to make it easier for estate vehicles to reach the loch, with fishing or forestry developments, or both, in mind. The landscape has been spared not one moment's thought.

I walked on down to the calming influences of the wood, the loch, and sat in the lee of the old ruin with its curved wind-cheating corners and its chimney stack miraculously intact. I thought then of all the centuries of human life here at Dalavil, at Caradal across the glen, and how it had all been achieved without a road other than the track worn by the centuries of the passage of feet. I thought of how the absence of a road was offered as the official excuse for not building a school here which could have kept Dalavil alive –

perhaps it would have been living still in the way that Elgol is living still with its school playgrounds a few feet above the stony shore of Loch Scavaig. Well, now Dalavil has got its road rather more than a hundred and twenty years too late to help its people.

But in those intervening years Dalavil has grown wild, and its wilderness too is a thing of no meagre consequence. The road that is too late for Dalavil's people is now a thunderous intrusion on Dalavil's wildness. Those susceptible elements of nature, it seems, are facing eviction too. One landowner's convenience put the Dalavil people out of their houses and off the land they had worked, fashioning agriculture out of wilderness; now, after more than one hundred and twenty years, how little has changed.

There were four whooper swans on the loch, a quarter of a mile from where I sat, their voices carrying quietly, fitfully, on the sea wind. The eagles were in the air as I trudged east again giving the wretched road as wide a berth as I could. If I ever come back to Dalavil (perhaps threading a perilous course up the shore from the lighthouse track) I wonder if there will still be swans and eagles, I wonder how much wildness I will find. One more sanctuary has got its plight, and the Garden of Skye grows one more strain of melancholy.

Chapter Five

A Life in a Landscape

THE DIRTIEST trick the Ordnance Survey maps play on Skye is to split ninety per cent of the Island into two maps and hive off the remaining ten per cent to the mainland, lumping it in ungraciously with Kyle of Lochalsh and its surrounds. In particular, this crude division of landscapes severs Isle Ornsay, the small tidal island off Sleat's north-east shore, from Isle Ornsay, the shorebound township named after its small tidal island. So the OS achieved what the sea failed to achieve, and you can still wander muddily over for an hour or two either side of low tide, stepping gingerly as a heron.

The name is confusing. There are several islands around the Hebrides and the Northern Isles called Oronsay, but Ratcliffe Barnett claims that the derivations are very different:

This island, despite the fact that there are the ruins of an ancient chapel on it, is not named after Saint Oran, like the Island of Oronsay which lies off Colonsay, (it should be explained that the suffix 'ay' is Norse for island and very evident in Orkney and Shetland place names). Both of these islands are called after saints – Colonsay after Columba and Oronsay after Oran. But the word Ornsay is a place description pure and simple. The island is called in Gaelic Eilean Diarmid or Diarman, which easily becomes Eilean Tiarman, a corruption of Eilean Tioram, or Dry Island. Now, tioram is the Gaelic equivalent for the Norse word oras-ey, which means ebb-tide island. So Isle Ornsay is the island that is connected with the mainland at low tide – a very exact description of a place.

So it is, and the fact that today's Gaelic rendition is none of his listed alternatives but Eilean Iarmain merely shows how language is never still for long, and what a chancy business the whole game of unravelling ancient names really is, chancy but fun.

There is a modern house on the island as well as the scraps of St Oran's chapel, or the chapel which bears no relation whatsoever to St Oran, but by far the most conspicuous feature of the place is the lighthouse and its twin-gabled cottage. The lighthouse converses in bright whispers across the Sound with the lighthouse at Sandaig under Beinn Sgritheall. They are linked not just by sightline and the waters of the Sound but by one troubled life which found much solace and not a little adventure and misadventure in this landscape. Sandaig was the writer Gavin Maxwell's Camusfearna, immortalised in his three best-known books, and later in his life he owned and briefly lived in the lighthouse cottage of Isle Ornsay before moving into Eilean Ban's lighthouse cottage up the Skye coast at Kyleakin. The landscape symbolised by the two lighthouses of Isle Ornsay and Sandaig, and the otters which habitually grace both their shores, so permeated the lives and work of both Gavin Maxwell and the poet Kathleen Raine with whom he shared a tormented relationship, that anyone who has explored their writings will be struck by the power of the landscape and the role it played in shaping their lives together and apart.

I should pause here to say something of Maxwell's influence on my own life, not that I ever met him, but his writing infiltrated my mind at its most impressionable age and has ever since been a source of wonder and admiration for me, and one of which I never tire. During my late teens and early twenties, an improbably distant era now from the vantage of mid-forties, I became headily smitten with the awareness of my Scottishness and the tapping into an innate but distant Celtic strain of blood. I quested among my instincts for tangible rocks to cling to within all these dreamy intangibles which bestrew some of Scotland's less credible and over-romanticised cliches. As part of the process I devoured books about Scotland, choosing titles which appealed to me for the heady ring of a taut phrase on a dust jacket of mountain and loch and island. Needless to say, I blundered through much exquisitely-titled trash, but in the midst of it all, a few titles bore me true and pure riches. Two books in particular have served like beacons – or lighthouses for that matter – through all the intervening years of my life. One was George Mackay Brown's *An Orkney Tapestry* and the other was Maxwell's *Ring of Bright Water*, and no year passes in which I do not read them both, in whole or in part. I have since delved into the work of both writers in great detail, but Maxwell's is the landscape addiction I succumbed to, and he writes landscapes like no-one else I ever read. Nor are his powers restricted to this corner of Scotland, and I believe the best of all his writings lie in his books about Iraq and Sicily, where landscapes and peoples are evoked with immense power and emotion and sensitivity.

It was here though, in a land-and-seascape illuminated by two lighthouses that he unfurled a distinguished literature which captured and continues to capture millions of readers across the world. He is perhaps yet to be accorded his full due as a writer, but his books still sell and sell, and at Sandaig in particular, discreet pilgrims are forever wandering his shore and sitting by his waterfall above that ring of bright water which curves in a glittering arc to the sea. I am among them.

Somewhere before 5am on that February morning of the muted curlew airs, the thin shriek of heron, the falsetto gibberish of the oystercatchers and the Isle Ornsay otters for company, I remembered another such dawn autumns ago, camped under Beinn Sgritheall. That night too was a sleepless one, punctuated by the same sounds (with the addition of stags' throats pouring anthems across the Sound) and roofed by the blackest sky and the most startling show of stars I ever saw. I climbed through that dawn, and the day's first sunlight threw my Brocken Spectre onto the summit clouds of Beinn Sgritheall. Near the summit, a thin snake of water spills from boulders, flirts with underworld and the overworld for a couple of hundred yards then careers down the mountain to the sea, 3,000 feet in a mile. In the process of its giddy journey it cleaves a dark gorge in a hidden waterfall. Maxwell called that fall 'the soul of Camusfearna', for its sound was the perpetual voice of his home. It is the same burn which then curves across Maxwell's shore, fringed by alders, in a ring of bright water to the sea. So when I first discovered the source of that water, the Allt Mor Santaig, and followed it downhill to Maxwell's Camusfearna, it was more than mere water I pursued.

That was my first pilgrimage and it drew me a little deeper into Maxwell's work and his landscape. There was a second pilgrimage which enmeshed me in it forever, the following September.

It was, if such a thing exists, a God-given day. It was as though nature had paused in that early September no-man's-land between summer and autumn and meshed something of both seasons into a golden lull which was neither of them. All the strewn fineries of the land wore their brightest seductions, a bazaar of nature, the golden Skye bird sunned its crooked wings and the Sound of Sleat was a sash of creased silk. From the smoky skin of a first frost on my tent at dawn until the last snuffed sunset flame, Maxwell's world held still and quiet, a day harvested by nature for herself.

I sat alone in its midst, my mind rummaging through Maxwell's life there and those traits of my own life which had lured me there and now lured me back. It was then that I became aware of three silhouettes across the bay, black against the gold glare of light, a man, a boy, and what looked like an awkwardly running dog. They paused at the bay's furthest edge and the sound of voices carried clearly across the stillness, although I could make out no words. I grew vaguely irritated at their presence because it has stemmed the free flow of my thoughts, even at such a distance. When I am alone in such a place I like to be *alone* there.

The three figures passed briefly out of sight behind a low rise in the ground and I watched for them to re-emerge beyond it. They did not re-emerge, nor did they retrace their steps. After a few minutes I crossed to the place, mild irritation tempered by unease. There was no trace of anyone having been there – no sound, no footprint, no swimming figures in a square mile of sea, nothing. The thought lodged, and it remains neither accepted nor dismissed that the 'awkward dog' was an otter. There was a time on that shore when the silhouettes of a man and a boy and an otter walking together would have been as familiar as the rocks and the sand and the curve of the burn. Weeks later, I would discover that I had seen my phantoms ten years to the day after Maxwell's death. I felt as if he had tapped me on the shoulder.

So now when I sit amid the pre-dawn rocks of Isle Ornsay with the moon sunk and no brighter lights in all that sea-and-landscape than the gossiping lighthouses of Sandaig and Isle Ornsay, it is Maxwell who comes into mind again. I remember some words he wrote after his first encounter with the place as a prospective buyer:

It was as though I had found Camusfearna once again, the same sense of sudden freedom and elation, the same shedding of past mistakes and their perennial repercussions. Here, it seemed to me, where the rocks and the white stone buildings were the only solid things in a limitless bubble of blue water and blue air, one might be able to live at peace again, to recover a true vision long lost by now in the lives of other humans and in the strifes of far countries; here one might set back the clock and re-enter Eden.

But Gavin Maxwell's life would never be as simple again as the day he walked alone into the primitive embrace of Camusfearna. Eden was as elusive here as he (and others, for his path was strewn with Eves and Serpents) had ensured it had become at Sandaig across the Sound. He acknowledged as much immediately:

> I did not know . . . that you cannot buy paradise, for it disintegrates at the touch of money and it is not composed solely of scenery. It is made of what many of us will never touch in a lifetime, and having touched it once there can be no second spring, no encore after the curtain falls. This is the core of our condition, that we do not know why nor at what point we squandered our heritage; we only know, too late, always, that it cannot be recovered or restored.

There was a third pilgrimage to Sandaig, years later, during a haphazard exploration of that West Highland shoreline, in which I found myself, almost unsuspecting, back in Sandaig Bay where I met again the unrepentant waters of the Allt Mor Santaig. The passion of that unstoppable water of such mountain sweetness lapsing at last into the overwhelming salt bitterness of the sea seemed somehow to encapsulate all that Maxwell and Kathleen Raine sought here: there had been much sweetness, all consumed at last by the overwhelming salt of a Fate which seemed to plague Maxwell's life and taint his best endeavours.

> All that wandering year
> I walked by waters:
>
> Spring was the Allt Mor Santaig
> weaned at Sgritheall's breast

still mad with summit snows
as it tried to sweeten the sea.

Summer I swam among islands
sunned and lulled by enchantment's distance
blind to the warning light
a-flicker on Eden's shore.

Autumn a dark and troublesome river
among fiery rowans; spates
plucked away one luckless tree
still blazing.

Winter an ocean gray
on gray with fast storms
water at its utmost. There
where I walked

along the frayed edge of the land
I chanced on a honeyed stream
lapping with bright and vivid tongues
at all that oceanic salt.

It was the Allt Mor Santaig
a year older but no wiser.

Isle Ornsay for me will always be two shores, the one that lies in
the lee of Sleat's eastern slopes, the other the shore it contemplates
across the Sound where Beinn Sgritheall rises primevally, and
where a far lighthouse, a curve of white sand, and a ring of bright
water commemorate a life which belonged utterly to its landscape,
where among all its torments it found a brief era of peace.

Chapter Six

The Shadow of the Cuillin

IT IS some shadow. The two mountain ranges of the Black Cuillin and the Red Cuillin would each be startling enough without the other. That they should both be crammed into the same ten-mile-wide coast-to-coast Island wedge is one of nature's most outrageous overindulgences in all Scotland.

The shadow of the Cuillin has impressed man ever since it was the exclusive preserve of a few herdsmen who might know its glens and passes and corries but not its summits. It falls mightily on a ring of Skye communities from Elgol to Broadford to Carbost, and from offshore Soay it is a gaunt bulwark which curtains off the rest of the world. It consumed for centuries the imaginations and sorely tried the vocabularies of a species of writer-travellers who never let their haverings be tempered with thoughtful exploration or even accuracy. It was still going on when Sir Walter Scott stumbled onto the shore of Loch Coruisk, and with his reputation as a romanticist to sustain, produced a scribbled overblown gibberish which was inevitably enough to set in motion a cavalcade of gawping, primitive tourism.

Finally, the shadow of the Cuillin shrouded the waking moments of mountaineering man throughout his most impressive golden age in Scotland. All that Scott and his predecessors misrepresented came under increasingly closer scrutiny through the second half of the nineteenth century until three remarkable men let their enlightenment play on the shadow and changed things forever.

The attractions were twofold – the striking sea-girt mountain shapes of the Black Cuillin and the fact that the rock is gabbro. Gabbro is wondrous stuff to climb on and although it can turn a new pair of leather boots into papier mache in a fortnight and turn a climber's hands into a crossword puzzle grid of lacerations, it gives that glorious adhesion in intimate contact which pumps the adrenalin of confidence into a climber's being so that he casts aside his old ideas of limitations and inhibitions and dares beyond his dreaming. If sometimes he dies in the process, what then? One man who was in no doubt was the first Cuillin mountaineer who made a name for himself in pursuit of climbing for the sake of climbing. Sheriff Alexander Nicolson wrote: 'The loss of life is a small thing compared with the full and free exercise of our powers and the cultivation of a bold, adventurous spirit; and any nation which has ceased to think so is on the fair road to decay and degradation.'

Nicolson was Skye born, at Husabost on Dunvegan Loch's west shore in 1827. He spent much of his adult life away from Skye, but it seems as if the Cuillin haunted him forever in the same way that the Pentlands were never far from the mind of Robert Louis Stevenson. He was, by all accounts, a much more accomplished Gaelic scholar than he was a law officer although his insistence that the name Cuillin is derived from A'Chuillin meaning holly, has been much discredited by subsequent theorists. The dissidents argue that holly is a scarce tree on Skye and that the allusion to the holly-leaf shape of the main Cuillin ridge is too fanciful for serious consideration. I am not so sure, but then I am no Gaelic scholar. Yet the Cuillin *in silhouette* have all a holly leaf's serrations and the leaf theory is particularly impressive if you see the mountains reflected in a lochan. Besides, in the Cuillin of all places, why shouldn't the name's derivation be a fanciful one? Here, after all, some of the mountains have been named after men, and what could be more fanciful than that?

Nicolson came home on holiday to climb in 1865, scampered up Sgurr nan Gillean, thereby cementing his childhood love of the Cuillin in climbing. Then in 1873, 'from Glen Brittle on a very stormy day he found his way to the lochan at the head of Coire Lagan and obtained out of the midst of driving mist a single glimpse of a great peak, one of the wildest objects he had ever seen'. What he had seen was the central peak of three summits collectively known as Sgurr Sgumain, but once he had become the first man to stand on its summit – the summit of all the Cuillin – it became Sgurr Alasdair, Alexander's Peak.

That assured his niche in climbing's hall of fame, but his finest hour was still before him. In 1874 he made the first ascent of Sgurr Dubh, arriving on the summit at sunset and descending to Coruisk in the dark and with a rug for a rope.

Nicolson blazed the trail then, but another Skye man was hard on his heels, and with him he would bring the Genius. The Skye man was a crofter, the other a noted academic. They were an unlikely partnership, but it is not overstating things to say that they changed the way men looked at mountains, and at the Cuillin in particular. The academic wrote of the crofter thus:

'He understands not only the joy of a hard climb but can also appreciate the marvels a beautiful mountain land is perpetually offering one.'

Joy?

Beauty?

In the feared Cuillin?

This was new! Here was nothing less than a prodigious leap in the awareness of wildest nature away from the mild hysteria of Scott and the others. It was based on the first-hand evidence of two people who had taken the trouble to explore at first hand all the sensations of the mountain landscape and to find stored beauty and challenge within the barrier of hostility which many perceived in the Cuillin at a distance. It was the hallmark of John Mackenzie of Sconser and Professor Norman Collie, director of chemical laboratories at University College, London. Mackenzie was born in the right place at the right time as far as the history of mountaineering was concerned. The shadow of the Cuillin falls on Sconser, and the boy born in that shadow went exploring first the Red Cuillin which were his doorstep, then the Black Cuillin beyond, and, so it is said, he climbed Sgurr nan Gillean at the age of 10. Even at that age, he was seeing not the frowning mountains which so many feared but their space and their brightness and their vision. He became the Cuillin's first real climbing guide, and it was as a guide that Collie sought him out.

Collie first came to Skye to fish and washed up at Sligachan in 1886, had his head turned by the Cuillin, and after the first few inquiries, he did the only thing a chap could do in the circumstances – he sent a telegram to London for a rope. After a few early failures in which he learned the problems of the Cuillin, he met Mackenzie and began a spectacular haul of the solutions. They climbed together every summer after that, and Collie's definition of summer grew ever more relaxed as it lengthened to much of the year outwith winter. They climbed together until they were too old to climb, and when Mackenzie died in 1934, it was the end of an association which had lasted for fifty years. Collie paid him this handsomest of tributes:

'He is the only real British Climbing Guide that has ever existed.'

Climber Ben Humble paid his own tribute to Collie in his book, *The Cuillin Skye*, the best of all books about the Cuillin and one of the best about any mountains anywhere:

Collie was over 50 by now; often he listened to discussion

about new routes but did not venture information. After those concerned had departed he would say with a chuckle: "If they *do* get there they'll find a cairn."

It was Collie's cairn of course. He was the Messner of his day, achieving the impossible almost as a matter of routine, setting the standards by which all the other great climbers of his day would have to judge themselves.

Humble added a telling footnote:

Some of the finest articles which have appeared in mountaineering club journals were from Collie's pen. He detested that type of article which gave times and distances like a railway timetable and failed to appreciate the wondrous beauty of the mountain scene.

Collie went on to climb all over the world, but the Cuillin were in his blood as they were in Mackenzie's, and despite the fact that they went into the Cuillin to climb, their attitude to the mountains was unlike that of many a mountaineer and closer to Tenzing's relationship with the high Himalaya: 'We are the mountains. The mountains are the bone. We are the blood'. It is fitting that the epitaph to Collie's era was a wonderfully unselfconscious tribute, a single paragraph which has gone into the literature of Scottish mountaineering, a small and much quoted masterpiece. I make no apology for quoting it again, for in my own small quest for the Heart of Skye, it evokes perfectly the last almost mystical days of one of the last to hear the Island heartbeat in the Cuillin before it grew inaudible under a new climbing era's clamour. The words are those of Richard Hillary, a young pilot who was to die – ironically before Collie – in the Battle of Britain. He had gone to Sligachan on what would be his last leave, in 1940.

We were alone in the inn save for one old man who had returned there to die. His hair was white but his face and bearing were those of a mountaineer, though he must have been a great age. He never spoke but appeared regularly at meals to take his place at a table tight pressed against a window, alone with his wine and his memories. We thought him rather fine.

A golden age of climbing had been born with Nicolson and died with Mackenzie and Collie. Perhaps in another fifty years from now, others will look back at the post-war climbers culminating in Messner's astounding ascents of all the world's 8,000-metre mountains and brand that a golden age. But Collie out-Messnered Messner because he defined mountaineering as he climbed. There was no tradition to build on, and climbing can never again produce his like, just as it cannot now produce another Messner. Too many climbers now know too much about climbing and too little about mountains. How many can claim as Humble wrote of Mackenzie that 'every peak and pinnacle were known to him, every corrie and lochan. He was a fount of knowledge in the matter of place-names; the ways of all wild things of the mountains were as an open book to him.'

And Humble points out:

Skye is the only place in Scotland where mountains are named after men. Hoary names they have – Sgurr Alasdair, Sgurr Thearlaich, Sgurr Thormaid and Sgurr Mhic Coinnich. And never were men worthy of giving their names to mountains than Sheriff Nicolson, Charles Pilkington, Norman Collie and John Mackenzie.

It is as well perhaps that Collie had no inkling of the fate that climbing would inflict on the Cuillin, and the way it has since swamped Sligachan where he died and Glen Brittle which he surely haunts.

Chapter Seven

The Valley of the Ancients

EVEN NOW, with a smothering of the wrong kind of forestry and a spaghetti junction of power line pylons, there is still an indefinable air of antiquity about that meeting of roads by the Broadford Hotel. Beinn na Cailleach, the Hill of the Old Woman, is the hovering presence which sustains the idea, that and the fact that the lesser of the two roads vanishes south-west almost at once, vanishes, but so obviously aims at the mountains and the ocean coast of the Island, that from the very first I have thought of it as a way back into the embrace of an older Skye.

The legend, if legend it be, of Beinn na Cailleach assists the thought process. It says that the mountain's vast summit cairn marks the burial chamber of an eighth-century Norse princess who lived at Castle Maol, that fragment of a remnant which lords it timelessly over the impatience of Kyleakin's ferry queue. Her death wish was to lie where she would feel the breath of her native winds, and her people so revered her that they went to astonishing lengths to honour her wish, and conferred on her an immortality unmatched by any of Skye's countless heroes.

So on a day when the black wind of mourning was scudding down the northern seas, a unique cortege wound up the mountain's sheltered southern slopes, climbing through the steepening bouldery flanks until at last it stepped onto the broad and domed summit and into the wind she craved for its northern fragrance. The mountain top had been aswarm with labouring for days, weeks perhaps if the Princess' death was signalled by long illness or tribal portent, but there is never enough time to build a burial cairn. Hand-picked young men from the Princess' tribe heaped the great cairn, with perhaps a tribal elder to oversee the thing, to see that it was shaped well, to advise on the set of stone on stone, and perhaps they laboured on still as the others drifted away quietly down the mountain, heads bowed, salt-eyed. The men stayed on the mountain until it was done, while others fetched and carried up and down the mountain, satisfying their every need, for it was no meagre work then to have heaped such a monument to such a Princess on such a mountain. These were legend builders. Perhaps for weeks, then, there was a desultory procession up and down and all across the mountain . . . The folk below would see the great cairn rise and wonder at it all. For sure, they would not contemplate that twelve hundred years later, others would consider the evidence of their labours and marvel – at their skills, their courage, their devotion, and at the nature of the woman who inspired it all.

In return for such lavish tribute, the Princess' spirit would care for her people whenever danger threatened. How diligent a guardian she proved to be is not recorded, but certainly her chosen summit is the guardian of her people's landscape so that they could evoke her and draw courage from her every time they raised their heads, and perhaps that was all the guardianship they needed.

And willing scrutineers of legend should consider the following:

Beinn na Cailleach also stands sentinel at the entrance to that mountain-hugging valley which wanders south-west to the ocean, a swathe clear through the Island and clear through the Island's history and prehistory. Skye has nothing else like Strath, a necklace of ancient sites, stone circles, cairns and other burial places which lean against the mountains, sheltered deep in the shadow of the Cuillin and perpetually in their thrall. In particular, many of them contemplate Skye's one great individualist mountain, and for me the most hypnotic mountain profile in all Scotland – Bla Bheinn. If they were inclined to place their Gods or whatever spirits they held to on mountain summits, none of the ancients of Strath would have far to look for their spiritual sustenance. With its draped ermine of spring snow or haloed by sea mist or garlanded with storms, Bla Bheinn from Strath is a fit abode for primitive Gods.

The valley ends at Elgol, where nature has orchestrated such a profile of the Cuillin ridge that it forms the journey's end of all Skye's journey's ends. To turn south-west at Broadford was never a journey to be taken lightly, and if the oldest of Strath's human relics predate the Princess by many centuries, it is as intriguing to consider what has befallen Strath since her death as that which went before. The last one thousand years of Skye's history is dominated by two names and all their lands – Macleod and Macdonald. (I still carry the vivid memory, part grimace, part grin, of my first visit to Skye and the obligatory tour of Dunvegan Castle: seven or eight of us were in the dank and darkened dungeon room, contemplating the hole in the floor where countless Macdonalds languished and awaited their doom, and while the guide spoke quietly and feelingly of how the Macleods and the Macdonalds had been 'bitter enemies for hundreds and hundreds of years' an American woman chimed nasally from our midst, 'Waal, ah'm half Macleod and half Macdonald so they must have gotten together sometime!'). The curious thing about Strath was that for all its strategic worth – a wedge clear across the Island with sheltered anchorages at either end and an ancient tradition as a sacred place – it never became either Macdonald or Macleod land. It was Mackinnon country, and in the protracted cross-fertilisation which would inevitably follow in the wake of Viking domination of their strongholds with Gaeldom, it does not take too much imagination to infiltrate the Cailleach's waning tribe with an emergent and distinctive clan, nor to adapt the legend of the Norse Princess so that her guardianship extended to whatever evolution her people followed in the lands where she once held sway. Certainly the Mackinnons of Strath seemed to lead a charmed life while their celebrated neighbours hacked and massacred their way into the clan's hall of infamy. Otta Swire makes the point well in her book, *Skye – The Island and its Legends*:

> Most clans had some nicknames usually uncomplimentary, bestowed upon them by others: "Murdering Macdonalds", "Treacherous Campbells", "Stab-in-the-back Macleans", and such. The Mackinnons of Skye were known as the "Two-faced" and no doubt they had need to be! Clever, tactful, and brave they must have been to remain in possession of their own land through the centuries. They married Macleods and they married Macdonalds, they spoke fair and were of service to both, and yet remained always independent.

It was perhaps no accident, not if the Mackinnons of Strath were sustained in their individuality by a strong measure of Norse blood, heirs of the Princess who was to be their guardian from the summit of Beinn na Cailleach. The landscape and the history of Strath are unique in Skye, and so is the legend of the Princess. If it has a measure of substance to it, surely the heirs of the legend might walk taller because of it. We have lost touch with such things, and there is little for us to do but guess. The guessing can be swayed, however, by the cairn on Beinn na Cailleach which is extraordinary for its size and its conspicuous site when most of Skye's summits have small cairns placed by mountaineers. *Surely* here is a monument to *someone*? That the Gaelic-speaking heirs of the faded

Norse regime set some store in what we now call legend is borne
out by another fragment of evidence: it is that while many of
Skye's summits still retain their Norse names, the mountain you
might think would be the most irresistably Norse of all has a Gaelic
name – Beinn na Cailleach.

It is Beinn Dearg rather than Beinn na Cailleach which dwarfs
Cill Chriosd, the most durable of all the sacred places of Strath.
However many eras of burials may lie beneath all that is visible at
Cill Chriosd now, there is no doubt that its role as a burial place is
ancient, nor that its name meaning the Churchyard or the Burial
Place of Christ is far from the earliest name by which the place was
known. Many tribes worshipped here and doubtless many gods
were invoked before St Columba sailed persuasively by,
proclaiming his own brands and definitions. The littered evidence
of his pagan predecessors is all along the valley and all around Cill
Chriosd – kirkyard stones which defy scrutiny, a stone circle, a
mysterious mound, and much more around the reedy and swan-
loud Loch Cill Chriosd along the road.

It has been a long, still and blousy day, leaden gray and warm
but refusing to rain anything but midges. There are downpours of
midges, cloudbursts of midges, and in between the downpours and
the cloudpours there are persistent drizzles of midges. My day has
been a silent and solitary trudge among the Red Cuillin, carving
through the mists of summits and shoulders having misplaced my
faith in an errant weather forecast. It has been hard going for the
toll such a day takes on the hill mind. Nature is away somewhere
else. The only wildlife is underfoot – saxifrages (various), orchids
(various), lizard (the only other moving creature on the hill; I greet
it like base camp greeted Hillary and Tenzing on the way down).
The hills feel empty, bloated, weary. I have long since decided my
day would have been better spent otter-watching on a wild treeless
headland, or prospecting for mountain avens and other startling

flowers among the secret crannies of an equally startling outcrop of Durness limestone across the valley. Anything but this high purgatory. Enough! I consult my compass hand and follow it down.

At five hundred feet the mist relents. Below me is the familiar shape of Cill Chriosd, a hard and angular presence in my day of shapelessness. Is it for that reason alone it beckons? I gatecrash a forest plantation on the shortest-distance-between-two-points principle and curse it fluently for its thoughtless imposition on this dearest of landscapes. There *were* trees here – look, there are a handful of descendants across the valley, oak and ash mostly; see how they fit the landscape, see how this monstrous regiment of conifers denies it!

The river is at its lowest mid-June dawdle, an easy wade. I pause in mid-stream to drown one more midge cloudburst by immersing my head in a pool. As I straighten up with head, neck and shirt drenched from river water and sweat, I am struck – it is the right word – by a fast gust of cool air. The force and the surprise catch me off balance, and suddenly I am sitting in the same pool, knocked over by the wind on a windless day. I stand again, tentatively to find that a steady breeze has blossomed in the wake of the assault, pressing my shirt coldly against me, but such is the cooling magic of wind and water that I turn to the Cailleach far back over my shoulder and shout, 'Thanks, Old Woman!' I wander up to the ruin, basking in the breeze as I walk. It is a delectable air, fragrant and a touch on the cool side of warm, and I begin to wonder if anyone has ever got drunk on a wind before. I swallow it in gulps, in pints, litres even.

The chapel ruin is roofless, the walls furred darkly with ivy and cotoneaster like quaintly overdone plaster, the kirkyard (the Gaelic *Cill* is better, signifying burial place whether church, Christian, or otherwise) this Cill is undoubtedly all three) quirkily punctuated (for Skye) with those heartless dark cypresses so beloved of urban

55

cemeteries. Here they are stunted runts, tormented by the Skye weather and about as appropriate as gum trees. I put my back to a warm stone and look at the shrouded hills again, but these few heady moments of wind have already begun to transform the land. The wind is in about the corries and baring mountain shoulders. The mist froths into bulbous overhangs, blossoms, withers and vanishes. The wind pushes the frontier of the mist up and up. The hills brighten and advance a pace as though a great burden has been shed.

I have sat here (or hereabouts) facing west, as I am sure the ancients did, poring over the profile of Bla Bheinn. If you know Bla Bheinn only as a mountain to climb, jammed between the Black Cuillin ridge and the blunt thrust of the Red Cuillin, you bypass the mountain's greatness. But if you were to build stone circles or chambered cairns or duns or brochs or burial grounds, choosing your site for its significance in the landscape, and if this was the valley you chose to build in, you would have built so that your quick and your dead deferred in worship and in death to Bla Bheinn, the landscape's godliest gesture. See how it always looks too massive for its own containing valleys as though it was about to burst out of its own landscape strictures. I have climbed Bla Bheinn several times and the mountaineer in me reveres it, but the landscape watcher in me holds it higher, because the *sanctity* of the mountain is appreciable only at arms' length, or so it has always seemed to me. If people anywhere in Scotland ever achieved that state of kinship with the mountains of which Tenzing spoke, I believe it could have happened here, in Strath. It is to our shame, collectively and individually, and it is symptomatic of the fault I find in what the Cuillin have become in our eyes, that such a state of kinship is quite beyond our era.

So the pagan builders and stone-setters of Cill Chriosd built here for the same reason that I like to put my back to a warm stone and watch Bla Bheinn, and the Christians when they came merely usurped the site and changed the name, calling it for Christ, as doubtless the pagans in all their earlier guises called it after other deities.

Now the wind works its sorcery on Bla Bheinn, peeling away layer after layer of gray swaddlings, baring black buttresses of glittering rock, dusting the very puckered pow of old gods, unveiling the matchless skyline of Skye's matchless mountain. If tourism could organise this on a daily basis like Edinburgh's one o'clock gun, it would be a bigger draw than the Edinburgh Festival, the ultimate marketing spectacular. Mercifully it cannot, and the spectacle remains the privilege of chance encounter, the reward for those who have suffered and survived trial by ordeal, the ordeal of the midge deluge. But it is no meagre reward, whatever the sufferings.

The sky begins to shred and that coy stranger, the sun, throws a single slanting ramrod of white light clear across the face of the mountain. Sky and mountain are still predominantly gray, and there is only vivid colour where the sunshaft alights, a fiery spotlight of yellow-green, the shade of early summer which the Island had somehow mislaid. For a few minutes that solitary beam upstages the mountain, then a second shaft bores through, then a third, and soon the sun is at the heart of a shifting fan of white light. New warmth floods the valley as the gray drains from mountain and rock and river, and colour overwhelms. The careful stones of the ancients and the bones they commemorate grow gratefully and briefly warm.

Sitting alone, and with most of my clothes strewn on the grass to dry, it is easy to succumb to the idea of a kind of primeval thrall, an elemental bondage rooted in man's earliest instincts, a thing of prehistory when he was as wild as the eagle. It is not a definable thing, not now, possibly not then; it is not as simple as sun-worship (surely a fraught and piecemeal doctrine for a climate like Skye's!) or mountain-worship, because there is no thread of continuity reaching back to clutch at. Besides, the conditions for its thoughtful contemplation arise so rarely now in the shadow of the Cuillin for the solitude and the silence on which it thrives are rare commodities and growing rarer. I try to focus the moment, setting this specific time against timelessness, sifting a single pure train of thought from a morass of thought. What I seek from such moments is a primitive communication with the great forces of nature – here and now these are the sun, the mountain and that perplexing wind. The only response I fancy I detect in nature is that it eggs me on to explore such trains of thought. As I watch the landscape unfold and the mountains reconstitute themselves out of their shrouds and back into their old familiar skyline shapes, my mind turns back to that first deadlock-breaking blore of wind which dumped me in the river. I begin not just to feel the wind but see it, as if it were a thing of shape and substance. It has crossed the sea in a tight and disciplined fleet, like Columba, bearing Gospels. It has brushed Rum, perhaps, restless for quest. It has fingered Rubh' an Iasgaich, westmost shoreline of Sleat, and Rubh' Aonghais which is southmost Soay. Finally it has compacted and beelined between Tarskavaig Point on the Sleat shore and Rubha na h-Easgainne of Strathaird, made landfall at Suisnish (reversing a grave tradition of embarkation at that grim landmark of the Clearances) and swerved into the sacred valley of Strath.

There it fanned out to fill the valley behind that vanguard thrust centred on Loch Cill Chriosd and the Broadford River where it travelled unhindered until our paths collided in midstream and I was forcibly baptised. How different is that wind from such as Columba and every other bearer of new conviction who has wandered this way, pausing for the duration of their own fleeting mortality to build their tributes to their gods or spirits or sun-and-mountain overlords – whatever? The difference is in the immortality of this wind preaching gospels of nature. When our own tribe has finally run its race and all our gods are piles of dust, that wind, that gospel, will sound nature's anthems here. It was doing so before Skye broke its land bridge with the Highlands, before the ice shuddered among the Cuillin and redefined them, before the first humble stone-carver set foot on the new Island. My hope for that far distant future time is that that same wind is heard by keener ears than ours.

Chapter Eight

The Hare and the 'Heb'

THE HEBRIDEAN Hotel's window on the world is streaked and strafed with the kind of rain the Island specialises in – a stiff and sodden summer breeze. The window opens with some difficulty and confronts me with a stark option: wide open or shut. It is midsummer night and the breeze means no midges, so I opt for wide open. At once the air rushes in, a balm of Cuillin and sea and haddock and chips. 'The Heb' as all Broadford and much of Skye knows the place, is a focal point kind of establishment.

The main road rumbles fitfully below, the bay across the street is the rest of the world. A brief army convoy is doing the rumbling tonight. A forestry truck (laden symbol of one more thoughtless land use regime in Skye's long repertoire of thoughtless land use regimes) adds its weight. There are desultory cars and caravans and coaches and various drop-outs from that ubiquitous tribe of tired vans which seems to haunt the less populous parts of Scotland, snuffed-out Transits, caved-in Commers, that kind of thing. A coach that says 'Skye-Ways Travel' on the side pauses at the hotel door. Its one alighting passenger calls a Gaelic goodnight to the driver from the pavement. That kind of coach I can live with.

There is one essential difference between such fitful traffic and traffic in most other places. It is that between vehicles or groups of vehicles there are long silences into which the sounds of shoreline nature rush – oystercatcher inevitably, curlew, gull, the rare cackle of admirably silent shelduck. It is then that you realise again that this road between Portree and all three of Skye's mainland ferries is the skinniest of island-skirting ribbons, and that its clinging townships, which are all so many travellers see of the place, turn their backs on the living, breathing, heart-beating mass of the Island. A few of Skye's roads penetrate deep within: this is not one of them.

The rain-polished road and the rain-dulled foreshore are all that the evening's weather has left in clear focus. I know this shore. Over there should be the Princess' mountain, Beinn na Cailleach, and unseen Strath; out there should be Applecross, the Crowlins, the steep, blunt stern of Scalpay, but there is only the sea-scudding rain, drifting and dragging opaque gray curtains down the dipping headlands to the wave tops. The sea's gray is almost charcoal, but a rim of almost white more or less delineates the shores of Scalpay and Longay. Above the white there are only dark and fluctuating blurs, nothing so tangible as an island shape. Pabay is a harder-edged lower-slung profile, closer at hand and with a stuttering frieze of trees across its low summit like a comb with teeth missing. My eyes work across what is left of the landscape, restless for the want of something to rest on, vague as the gray rain.

Skye does this, sometimes for weeks at a time, wraps itself in sodden cocoons of listless shrouds. The natives have long since learned the trick of turning their backs to it all and averting their eyes from its maddening hypnotism and so get on with life's daily ritual tasks with only a disgruntled shrug at the weather, a communal complaint over a dram in the Heb. I have never learned the trick. My work and my ritual tasks lie in the landscape. Skye's landscape is the most compelling I know, and always in days like these I want to be out in the clinging grayness trying to part the wet curtains to reassure myself that the landscape still lies where I last left it (can that single hung rainsheet really conceal *all* Bla Bheinn?). Eyes drift on trying to fathom the unfathomable gray from the window.

Suddenly a focal point stomps into view from behind the leafy bulk of sycamore tree in a shoreline garden. A low-tide rim of runnelled mud cuts off the street from the sea, the realm of shelduck, a swan-goose kind of creature in handsome technicolour. It is a drake which steps forward, hunting in the mud at a brisk goose-step, recognisable by the cherry-ish embellishment to the base of his scarlet bill. The duck has also been loitering behind the sycamore and she steps immediately after him. The cellophane-thin veneer of rainwater on the mud is enough to give each bird an abstracted reflection, and in the hard colour-shapes of the real thing and the dogged pursuit of their reflections, a landscape-watcher's eyes find the consolation of a riveting focal point. The drake stands tall between feeding forays in the mud, more goose-like than duck-like by far, with mute-swannish overtones in the round knob on the bill. The basic bodily white is daubed with the thoughtful brushstrokes of nature as abstract painter – a neatly finished off dark-green head is common enough among drakes, but the chestnut-brown swirl which lies like a halter on back and breast then bisects the belly from breast to tail . . . that is an extraordinary trait of plumage. There is more brown in the secondary feathers of the wings, amid much black and blue-black, and the whole unlikely arrangement of pattern and colour and goose-shape moves purposefully over the mud on pale pink legs and feet. You mistake a shelduck for nothing. My window-watching eyes fasten onto the pair eagerly.

Some parts of the foreshore are wetter than others, so the birds' reflections come and go as they cross wetter and drier ground; the pattern shapes move two or three or four at a time as a result, each set of patterns reshaping fluidly as each bird cranes low to feed or stands erect to march on; a small and perpetually readjusting flotilla of colour on the surface of the evening's gray-brown mud-sea. An oystercatcher (plus reflection) lands nearby them for the purpose of agitating: the purpose behind the purpose is less clear. The querulous presence of the oystercatcher and the indifferent turned backs of the shelduck serve in their contrasting characteristic behaviour patterns to underscore the almost total silence of shelducks.

In half an hour, these two shelduck quarter the low tide, hide-and-seeking with their reflections, never out of my sight, while the weather eases up and a white flare begins to burn through the air above Beinn na Cailleach, or rather above where Beinn na Cailleach should be. A pallor of watered-down sunlight whitens the tidal pools and the rainy puddles and a rainbow leaps across the east shore of the bay, sizzling down into the sea of Pabay. The shelduck glitter in the light and in that moment my mind lurches back to old shelduck-watching haunts in East Lothian, an old winter on Aberlady Bay where a friend once called them 'porcelain', an adjective which seemed so irresistibly perfect that the two words porcelain and shelduck have been inextricably entwined in my mind ever since. The sunlight on Broadford Bay puts a glaze on the birds and the porcelain imagery is restored perfectly. A smile of recollection flicks over the window face.

The sun fizzles out and the eyes grow restless again, roaming the rest of the bay, loitering among the grasses of Glas Eilean, a small tidal island thick with grasses and nesting common gulls. The same grasses fringe the seaward side of the street and the walls and fences of shoreline gardens where the bay curves away from the street. Between the shore grass and the island grass lies the tidal mud like the overdone filling in an oozy sandwich, the sandwich from which the shelduck plunder an evening meal.

There is a quiet rhythm to the evening. Its pulse is the stop-and-start foraging of the shelduck (a pacy progress criss-crossing the same patch of mud many times), the swishing interruptions of traffic, the spatter of rain, the voices and splashing footfalls of the Heb's sporadic early evening clientele, the ragged woodwind of gulls, the staccato of oystercatchers. All these have their patterns of movement, things in their place, quiet components of any early summer evening around Broadford Bay, the world from the window of the Heb. Something stirs in a corner of an eye, something on the road, a new movement, a new and cautious rhythm, a small-dog-big-cat kind of presence which is palpably neither of these even before the window eye adjusts and brings it into focus. The rhythm is wrong for one thing, and now that its focus sharpens, so are the ears. It is a brown hare.

He is a big buck hare and he crosses the road, the Heb's car park, and pauses on the car park's further edge beside the rear wheels of a large white van. It comes as something of a surprise to find a hare on Skye at all, and it is certainly the first I have seen in 25 years of watching the Island landscape. The ground behind the hotel, a sloping confusion of croft and field and moor, is ideal hare habitat, but the shoreline seemed to offer neither picking nor shelter for a hare, and given the additional hazard of the road and the disturbance of pedestrians, the expedition I now witness is just downright baffling.

A new voice calls a farewell from the bar door beneath, and new footsteps splash across the road to the car park. The van driver is about to reclaim his van. He has not seen the hare, and the hare gives no indication that he has seen the driver. By the time the driver reaches the van door he is no more than fifteen feet from the hare. The hare lopes beyond the back of the van, pauses again on the furthest edge of the car park to draw a paw across an ear. The engine fires and a cloud of diesel fumes drifts towards the hare, or rather it drifts towards where the hare has been a moment earlier. At the first syllable of the engine he is leaping down from car park to shore and crossing the mud towards the island at a flat-out gallop.

There are two obstacles in the hare's panic-path . . . the shelduck. He is no more than a yard from the nearest of the two when he swerves violently right to avoid it, only to put himself on a collision course with the second which he avoids with a four-footed skip to the left; without a backward glance he resumes his sprint to the island while the shelduck stand tall and still apart from their heads which slowly follow the frantic hare. Presumably they know each other. The van reverses, manoeuvres out of the car park, blocks out my view of the hare, and when its bulk and its noise have vanished and silenced, so has the hare. The shelduck feed on.

An hour later, I have closed my writing pad and my boots are following the clear hare tracks across the mud. The four-footed skip to avoid the second shelduck starts a new trail fully a yard to the left of the first one. Thereafter the hare's stride is unbroken clear over the mud to the island where it vanishes. There are still nesting gulls on the island so I resist the temptation to linger, but there is no sign of the hare and no obvious reason why the island's habitat should be more to his liking than the croft land behind the hotel. I asked around: it seems the animal is well known for its baffling offshore forays and has even been known to swim back . . .

Another squall cruises down from the Cailleach and flails the island. I thought she was supposed to protect her realm! Scalpay blurs, Longay trembles purply and unsubstantial in the last of the daylight. The Crowlin hint which emerged an hour ago has vanished again. A young gray wagtail perkily exploring a puddle careers out of control in the wind, as for a few dire seconds her head and tail point in the same direction, an uncanny curve which looks as wrong as it must feel. I wonder what happened to the hare.

Chapter Nine

The Corrie of Dreams

THE EASTMOST shadow of the Cuillin is its least tramped. The main road from the ferry to everywhere in the world north of Broadford inhibits exploration. It leaps and bounds and hairpins beneath the mountains, too close for thoughtful exploration, permitting only a couple of tourist whistlestops, until it disgorges mountaineering man and busloads of mountain-marvelling visitors at Sligachan. There is for sure much to marvel at – too much for any camera without a wide-angle lens. There must be more bad join-ups of over-lapped Boots prints showing that widest cross-section of the Cuillin from just above Sligachan than any other prospect in the land, but trying to match the mountains up is an old game and infuriating fun.

Between photographs you may spare a glance for that wide-shouldered, deep-chested, shallow-peaked mountain shape oddly cramped in the throat of Glen Sligachan. It recalls Bla Bheinn in the sense that it is an individualist wedged between two mountain herds, and that there seems to be insufficient room for it. The mountain is Marsco, and what with the gabbro superstars of Sgurr nan Gillean and the Harta Corrie across the glen, it should be overshadowed, but it catches your eye and holds it, a compelling focal point, the poor man's Bla Bheinn.

To mountaineering man, Marsco is usually stitched on to the end of a long high scree-strewn traverse from Glamaig (a much underrated highway with rare insights into the world of the black Cuillin across the glen), in which case he has spared no thought and no second glance for the unprepossessing corrie below him as he hurtles down the screes of Ciche na Beinne Deirge. Let him hurtle on then – for he is not ready for the Corrie of Dreams yet.

By the time the coast road has egged on its travellers to Sligachan where the world begins again, they have by-passed the Cuillin's most enigmatic portal, although if the Allt Coire nam Bruadaran is in good voice you may have paused briefly by the waterfall which propels it down into the most prosaic of concrete culverts and under the road. Below the road, the burn hirples through the flat machair-and-rock morass of the head of Loch Ainort, all passion spent. Years ago, when the only road worth the risk was the coast-hugging capillary by way of Moll and a suitably dignified stone bridge over the burn (this road itself a replacement for a much older road over the Druim na Cleochd), Sorley Maclean called a poem after this place. It is my favourite of all his poems. It sits well with my instincts because down at the head of the loch you are far enough away from the mountains to appreciate the significance of what it is you are far enough away from. But no-one before or since has appreciated it quite the way Sorley MacLean did. This is his *Kinloch Ainort*:

A company of mountains, an upthrust of mountains
a great garth of growing mountains
a concourse of summits, of knolls, of hills
coming on with a fearsome roaring.

A rising of glens, of gloomy corries,
a lying down in the antlered bellowing;
a stretching of green nooks, of brook mazes,
prattling in the age-old mid-winter.

A cavalry of mountains, horse-riding summits,
a streaming headlong haste of foam,
a slipperiness of smooth flat rocks, small-bellied bare summits,
flat-rock snoring of high mountains.

A surge-belt of hill tops,
impetuous thigh of peaks,
the murmuring bareness of marching turrets,
green flanks of Mossgary,
crumbling storm-flanks,
barbarous pinnacles of high moorlands.

There is no such place on the map today as Kinloch Ainort although the burn which joins the Allt Coire nam Bruadarach just above the stone bridge is the Abhainn Ceann Loch Ainort, the stream of the head of Loch Ainort. Besides, the map of a place like Skye and the importance or otherwise of its place names is forever changing, just as communities flourish and wither. I had been lured to this corner of the Cuillin, for example, not by the winter wildfowl in the loch or even Sorley MacLean's poem (although an impetuous thigh of peaks is irresistible enough!). I was lured instead by a name on the map. If you clamber above the waterfall rather than linger only long enough to fire off another barrage of snaps at it, you emerge into the widening girth of Coire nam Bruadaran itself, the tantalising Corrie of Dreams. But whose dreams? And dreams of what? My natural recourse in such circumstances is to consult the writing of Seton Gordon, but his timeless classic among the Island's literature, *The Charm of Skye*, was curiously silent. An explanation emerged a few years later when in 1937 he published *Afoot in Wild Places* and broached the subject briefly. He had gone as far as to ask an old man 'who had spent his life among the Cuillin hills and knew them better than any man, if he had heard the history of that place name, but he could tell me nothing of the vision that was dreamed in that lonely corrie which is so often shrouded in mist . . .' It was John Mackenzie, no less, and because Seton Gordon held him in the same regard as Collie and the rest, he concluded uncharacteristically for him that if Mackenzie didn't know, the search wasn't worth the effort. So if these two great Skye minds (the one the native who lived and breathed the place from birth till death, the other the famous and distinguished incomer who loved the place and lived at Duntulm for many years) could not uncover the tracks of the elusive Dreams, I felt quite justified in dreaming my own dreams here. Such a name as the Corrie of Dreams *should* have a legend after all, and surely a lingering exploration of the corrie would yield something to slake imagination's thirst?

It is an exhilarating water whose company you keep as you walk up into the corrie. The fall which so entrances roadside tourism is only the *coup de grace* of a quarter of a mile of steps and slides and staircases, jade pools and jacuzzis. Skye's mountain burns have a kind of surreal clarity at their best, the underwater rocks washed pale so that at even the flimsiest hint of brightness in the sky, the watercourse is a vivid alacrity, all sparks and satin sheens. In its shallowest, sunniest rock pools it can fool you into invisibility. You reach down to finger warm rock and your hand immerses to the wrist. A Skye burn is like no other you have encountered, and in the Corrie of Dreams, the burn is among the élite of that élite. Its rocks are the pink sandstone of the Red Cuillin, and on every hand the corrie walls speak to you in the same shade . . . except that high on a shoulder of Gars-Bheinn, sandstone and gabbro collide and merge in one monumental hinge. It would have been something to see, that forging of never-the-twain-shall-meet, in one great volcanic grunt.

A geography lesson slips into place here, for the headwall of the corrie is the 'side' of Marsco, but if you were to step from its dipped shoulder (the low point of the corrie skyline) onto the ridgey wiles of Gars-bheinn and traverse that prickly summit, you would confront another ridge which dips then soars blackly – Bla Bheinn. They are the same indivisible fraternity, the Red Cuillin and the Black, and their brotherhood throws the same great shadow across the Island.

Coire nam Bruadaran is wide and shallow, at first glance a place fit for daydreaming in at least, but turn after half a mile and see how it has gathered you in. Only the pale opal of Loch Ainort's seagoing waters reminds you of lesser lands below. Turn again and Marsco is suddenly a slung barrier, disappointingly shapeless from this side, but wearing a second small corrie high on one shoulder like a brooch. Coire nan Laogh is the Corrie of the Calves, and a more classically corrie-shaped corrie, perfectly sculpted in a single flawlessly curving shell-scoop, walls bulging like curtain folds: in the day's subdued light, a heavy gray-pink pastel curtain, subtly sensational. From here it might mask the entrance to another world, or an upper chamber of the mountain. What if the curtain could be parted . . . to walk inside the mountain, to climb Marsco from within, up through the very mountain core and emerge on the summit, that would be the stuff of a legend worth dreaming.

I had stopped to examine otter spraints by the burn, lifted my eyes from just in front of my feet to the high corrie in a single movement, servant to some inexplicable urgency with which my nature writer's instincts are sometimes blessed, found an eagle contouring inside the Corrie of the Calves. The bird emerged round that rim and began the long traverse of the Corrie of Dreams in that same impossibly slow flight technique I had seen orchestrated in Sleat. A glider pilot can do this – for about five yards before crashing. The eagle can do it until it runs out of hillside. Twice the bird landed on a rock, posed briefly, resumed the flight by stepping off and laying the width of its wings on the mountain air. Not once in the five minutes I watched it did the bird's wings beat, although occasionally a ripple would flicker through a wing tip like the widening wake which spills from a swimming otter.

The eagle leaned out into the space of the corrie rim. It made two fast circuits of the furthest corner under Gars-bheinn, drifting ever higher and clear out of the corrie, swinging into the teeth of the big winds which flayed Marsco's summit. Two more eagles hove to alongside, probably a family group, but there, dicing with the summit wind as it shredded a rag-and-tatter sky, gliding to a standstill (not hovering so much as hanging), they were a trinity with all the hallmarks and presence of Father, Son and Holy Ghost. It is easy to imbue your eagles with overlordly status in the Corrie of Dreams.

I wondered how the world *feels* from such an airy pedestal compared with (my closest personal experience) say, a day of limitless visibility on Bruach na Frithe; how different from the windless elixir of that summit as I knew it to know such a mastery of that mountain top element that it is of no account, to soar on a thousand feet higher than the summit, because the summit itself is of no account other than perhaps as a reference point; how different to know the means and possess the strength to stall and spin soundlessly in your own length, to rest on the air, to shape a shallow glide the length of the Minch and outstrip a peregrine falcon, or to fall a thousand feet with the air sculpting your face to your cheekbones (to have the summits rush up to you – there's an incomprehensible twist for a mere mountaineer!) then with perfect control, to check the fall and bounce a thousand feet back up.

The surprise of Coire nam Bruadaran was discovering shielings high on the corrie floor, yet perhaps it begins to make sense of the name. Often enough in Gaeldom, hill names derive from shielings or some event or characteristic in the shielings' story. We inherit the name; but all too often, because we no longer like to tell stories ourselves, the story behind the name is too long untold to survive. The shieling walls still stand waist high, thickened and furred with moss and turf. Among them is a series of five small roundish structures which look as if they might have been linked. One is a perfect circle. From their midst a woodcock rose and flew low and heavily, a dark, burdened lance, landed a hundred yards away and vanished in the instant. Take-off, flight, landing were all eerily soundless as if there were forces present which were not to be disturbed. Dreamers perhaps.

So it would seem that the dreams of Coire nam Bruadaran were dreamed by the shieling folk of Kinloch Ainort or Luib down by on the shore, and because every legend should begin with the words 'It is said' . . . without elaborating on who said, when they said it or under what circumstances . . .

It is said that there came a summer among the shielings of Coire Ceann Loch Ainort when the traditional high spirits of the young folk went too far. Among them was one Tormod Mor, only fourteen, but already brawny beyond his years and fearless, folk said, to an extraordinary degree. Hadn't he fended off the rogue wolf that had come about his father's place that previous spring, even snatching back a new-born lamb from the very jaws of the beast? Eye-witnesses said he seemed to use no force at all, that he almost seemed to persuade the wolf to drop the wretched thing and turn meekly away, but all Tormod Mor said was: 'He is not fierce, because he is a wolf.' Such courage in such a young man, they said, and because he was also fair and handsome and (said the Island Crone) destined for greatness, there wasn't a girl in all Skye whose head didn't turn towards him.

It was an idyllic summer, the weather the best folk could remember, the feeding good, the beasts prime, the evenings full of song and pipe and story and nudges and winks. Then it was midsummer night, when the darkness was nothing more than a gesture, a shrug of shadows on the east-facing corrie walls. A few of the younger men were jealous that Tormod was everyone's hero, and turned their high spirits and the fact that midsummer night was always an occasion to be marked in some way, into a small conspiracy, a practical joke which might also deflate young Tormod's status.

It was an hour before midnight that the singing and dancing and merry-making were interrupted by the distressed shouts of two young men as they came running down from high in the corrie. Tormod heard his name yelled out again and again. He came running to meet them, sensing adventure, primed, eager, just as they knew he would be.

'Tormod, Tormod,' they yelled again, breathless from their running. 'There are two calves trapped in the high corrie that's unclimbable – there on the ledge, look! They must have gone over from the top! You are the only one of us who could climb there. If anyone can save them, you can. It is all down to you. If we were to lower you down from the rim of the corrie . . .'

Tormod interrupted: 'I'll do it, the beasts look too young to be apart from their mother. We must reach them quickly.'

So, with the others shaking their heads behind his back or covering knowing smiles with their hands, the young men made for the high rim, lowered him down, as of course, they had already lowered the calves. In that hour of half dark, the last Tormod heard of them was the laughter and the taunts from above as they ran back down the mountain to the shielings, taking the rope with them. Their plan was to leave him there a few frightful shivering hours with the two demented calves, then go back in the morning and haul them all up to the appreciative laughter of the rest of the shieling folk. Tormod would emerge looking beaten and bedraggled, and may even have learned fear in the night, and the young girls would learn of this flaw in their hero and turn their heads elsewhere.

But no-one had counted on the storm. The young men were no sooner back in the shielings regaling the others with their escapade and swilling coarse whisky than it broke. There had been no sign of its approach, no storm-scent on the sea-wind. In an hour the corrie was a seething place of turbulent waters and banshee winds, and while there was suddenly real concern for Tormod on that high exposed ledge, the weather now precluded the slightest chance of reaching him. In any case, said the instigators, it will serve our cause the better, and the Tormod that we haul gasping over the rim of the corrie in the morning will have learned a deeper fear, and will surely have lost the calves.

On the mountain ledge, Tormod smelled the storm when it was still a mile down Loch Ainort, for he was not distracted by the shieling revelries and he was alive to every aspect of his predicament. He could see the shadow of the storm moving up the loch, and knew at once that the corrie was in its path. There was no shelter on the ledge, but a great rock showed an inch or two of space between it and the rock wall. If only he could move it.

Never was his strength so tested, yet never had he felt stronger. Long after he felt that his strength should have begun to fail him, he was still straining at the rock with tireless limbs. The gap widened an inch and still he strained at it. He paused for breath, then a remarkable thing happened. One of the calves brushed past him, put its muzzle to the crack and shouldered the rock aside. The second calf followed. Tormod was doubting his own eyes, but there was the rock, and the gap was now eight inches, the width the calf had squeezed through. He put his own shoulder to the rock as the storm broke. The great wind unbalanced him and thrust him viciously through the widening gap and into a deep warm calm. The boulder had guarded a cave. Then a voice spoke.

'You have entered the Sanctuary of Dreams. You will be a great leader of your people. Whenever you confront difficulty in life, the solution will come to you in a dream and you will awake with the knowledge you need to overcome all adversity.'

There was no obvious source of the voice, but it was an old woman's voice, and hadn't the crone prophesied greatness for him years ago. It seemed to Tormod in his bewildered frame of mind that the voice bore more than a passing resemblance to the old hag's voice. But certainly, there was only himself and the two calves in the cave. He knew now that he was safe, and in the cave's dry warmth, he slept until early morning. When he awoke, the calves led him up through a long spiralling tunnel until they brushed past one more rock and emerged among the summit rocks of Marsco and the tranquil summer sky paling in the north-east.

So it was that the shieling folk who had raced up the mountain in the aftermath of the storm found Tormod sitting on the summit, an arm round each of the calves' necks and grinning at his flabbergasted people in greeting. They marvelled at his escape, his skill, his strength, but all he would say was that he seemed to fall asleep, and that his dreams provided him with the knowledge to scale the mountain. It seems, he said, that in dreams, I have all the knowledge I need.

So Coire Ceann Loch Ainort became Coire nam Bruadaran, and the small high corrie where the rock hangs in curtain folds became Corrie nam Laoigh, which is the Corrie of the Calves, and just as Tormod's people only had his word for it all, you only have mine.

Chapter Ten

On Behalf of the Crofters of Gaeldom

Faisg air ácharn seo
air an 9mh Latha deug de'n ghiblean 1882
chriochnaich an cath a chuir muinntir a'Bhraighe
air sgath tuath na gaidhealtachd

Near this cairn
on the 19th of April, 1882
ended the battle fought by the people of Braes
on behalf of the crofters of Gaeldom

LATE JUNE, 110 years after the event, I stopped like many before me at the roadside cairn on the five mile cul-de-sac to Peinchorran where Loch Sligachan nudges into the Sound of Raasay. Why stop? I have no new wisdom in such matters, no insights to pronounce nor revelations nor researches. Yet among those who have gone before me, spreading insight and enlightenment, is Jim Hunter, writer, journalist, broadcaster, and thoughtfully articulate ambassador for crofters in general and Skye crofters in particular. His is the definitive study, *The Making of the Crofting Community*, but enough of your blood will boil if you read his devastating pages on the events of 1882 from his book *Skye, The Island*. I have read them often and always the blood boils, always the same lump in the throat at the dignified evidence of the crofters to the subsequent historic Royal Commission.

Why stop? Homage of a kind: I am first a writer for whom the landscape is raw material, which all too often means that the people in the guise of those who shape and control what happens to landscape are the enemy. That is not the case with crofting. I like the crofting landscape, like how it uses the land, like how it (mostly) works hand-in-glove with nature. I dislike (mostly) the big estates, the big landowners, land as currency, acres as playthings. I revile the abuse of landscape and the abuse of those who respect it and work it well, making only modest demands on nature. Rarely has there been worse abuse than was heaped on the crofters of Braes. So I stop.

I am also that species of Scot who inclines instinctively to the Celtic components in what we have become as race and nation, and with nothing more than a long-lost Irish ancestry and far-off hints of Argyll to explain it away. I am less moved by people than by nature (with a few honourable individual exceptions), but it is to such humble heroes as the crofters of Braes, 1882, that my heart goes out unbidden. If we had put our Highland and Island landscapes under crofting expansion to the same extent and with the same zeal that we have stifled it with dull forests, we would have a healthier landscape, a healthier diversity of wildlife, a healthier heritage, and crofters would not be clutching at straws and flirting with extinction – individually if not collectively. It is not too late, there has been much progress in recent years, but it is still much more difficult than it should be. Enlightenment has not loosened all the shackles with which the worst excesses of Highland land ownership have enchained a people and their place. So, for the Braes crofters instinctively and because this is Sorley MacLean's country and his poetry has elevated them and because Jim Hunter has elevated them and their cause in my mind, I stop. All that, and because on such a warm and glittering blue morning on such a shore which I love with such an intensity, it is a good thing to do.

There is a shelf of grassy clifftop across the road, and by selecting a heathery shelter with care I put the sun on my face and blunted the cooling edge of a northerly breeze. At my feet the Sound of Raasay trembled towards the sun as though a host of herring had suddenly surfaced, sensationally silver. A small rock islet a few hundred yards away was paved with birds: coy common gulls on late nests, sunning eider drakes, cormorants in all their unlikeliest heraldic stances. A red throated diver was feeding far out in the Sound, perhaps down from a high loch on Raasay where years ago I watched their stylish courtship from the luxury of my tent and the soft hiss of the stove brewing fresh coffee and the woodwind wail of the birds were the only sounds in the world. Hour after hour they circled each other and put their cries on the evening air, and in the barely dark May midnight, theirs was the last waking sound I heard. I did not lightly forget the red throated divers of Raasay.

Continuity in such a landscape takes many forms. The crofters of Braes today cannot be blind to the tradition in which they stand. They must pass the cairn every time they drive to the main road, every time they drive home. In their quieter moments, the crofters of 1882 and all their forebears and descendants would hear the same diver wail out on the Sound, the same clamorous gulls, the same baying seals; the sight of a school of dolphins cruising the Sound would stop them in their tracks and catch their breaths as one more sleek and shining school now stopped me in mine and prised free an involuntary gasp . . . all that blinks in the eye of the one sea.

Wave on darkening wave
the gull-loud Sound scoffs
at the frail rock-resistance
of the Island. These birds

are not the fruits
of a single season
but the single sea generation
the Island grew old in,
the sea-cries of all time.

The Island is likewise
the seedbed of all ploughshares,
our labours as seasonless as the sea,
all our colossal labours
prey to that old eagle, time.

All ploughs cut the Island skin
only as deep as the Island
lacerates the mouth
of each telling, darkening wave.

It is all no more
than a way of passing time.

A hundred and ten years here or there, then, is worth barely a syllable in the Island's story as nature tells it, and the belated cairn to the Braes crofters of 1882 is a futile timepiece in nature's scheme of things. So a few folk stood up to Lord Macdonald, corrupted ignorant bully that he was; so they finally declined to suffer one more indignity and withheld their rents, and when the laird sent the sheriff's officer brandishing a clutch of eviction notices they sent him away with a flea in his ear and a bruise here and there, then a fair imitation of hell broke loose. So what? When did men *not* fight among themselves? Yet a tide turned here too, a small tide and a slow one, but in its own way as inexorable as the sea and it flows still.

The Allt an t-Sithein is a very private Skye burn, and the waterfall which hurtles down to the north shore of Loch Sligachan is all that most people see of it, if they see anything of it at all. In much the same way as the Allt Coire nam Bruadaran conceals the Corrie of Dreams behind its waterfall, the Allt an t-Sithein deflects further exploration with a final flourish enjoyed primarily by dog walkers and other sundry patrons of the caravan and camp site at Sligachan. Why linger here when the superstar scope of the Cuillin spreadeagles the opposite shore of the loch? But whereas you can follow the Allt Coire nam Bruadaran every step of the way from source to sea loch with nothing more strenuous than the final steady plod up to the watershed on that dipped shoulder of Marsco, the Allt an t-Sithein is a toilsome expedition and one which is only feasible during that rarest of Skye phenomena, a drought. The name itself carries a hint of the difficulties; surely the Burn of the Faeries must stem from grottos and secret places?

I climbed on a hot, dry day, the last as it turned out, of thirty such consecutive days, and found the burn low and quiet, the fall half-hearted, the pools barely troubling their brims. A loosely formed plan to climb the hill above the fall by following the high bank of the burn all the way to the summit was abandoned when I realised that climbing in shorts and bare feet I might climb the burn itself, daring the grottoes and hidden falls and tunnelled depths of the watercourse.

The rock was warm, the pools cool, the scrambling idyllic. The only treacheries paved the beds of the pools and clung to the grotto walls, a slippery ooze unnerving to the touch of hand and foot. So I scrambled gleefully up and over the dry rock and where taking to the water was the only resort, I took to it cautiously testing every footfall and handhold. In this way I climbed easily and burrowed up through the twisty gorge, while its walls grew ever steeper, higher, darker.

Above one more waterfall the burn suddenly narrowed into a long, straight, black-walled, roofless tunnel. An image of a close in Edinburgh's Royal Mile crossed my mind, and for a few moments those twin variations on that single dark rock theme swam companionably there side by side. The closes were the instinctive rhythmic solution of centuries of stone masons to the fact of nature as architect in Edinburgh's Old Town, stone-flagged tributaries to the Royal Mile's tumbling riverbed of gray setts, and offering furtive glimpses of the Old Town's old rock soul. The one urban environment I have ever loved had its echo-in-nature here on a Skye hillside. I paused by the tunnel mouth, turning over that idea in my mind, thinking of half a dozen dark entries all bearing the name 'Close' – Advocates, Bakehouse, Brodie's, Fishmarket, Fleshmarket, World's End – each beckoning with its own hidden promise of insights and stored secrecies. All that was missing here was a carved lintel – 'Faeries Close'.

Something else had assisted the association in my mind between this Skye hillside and Edinburgh's old rock citadel. Back in 1882 and the following spring, that same Advocates Close would echo to the footfalls of lawyers and civil servants whose minds were well exercised by events centred on this same Skye hill. For this hillside so deftly and darkly explored by the Allt an t-Sithein is a flank of Ben Lee, of which Jim Hunter wrote:

> Ben Lee, at well under half their height, is not one of the island's more self-evident rivals to the Cuillin. In the early part of 1882, however, had you asked the average southerner to name a peak in Skye, Sgurr Alasdair and Sgurr nan Gillean would have posed no challenge whatsoever to Ben Lee; for the previously obscure issue of the Ben Lee grazings was then at the centre of an increasingly impassioned national debate and the not infrequently dramatic doings of the inhabitants of Peinchorran, Balmeanach and Gedintailor (collectively the Braes) were being chronicled daily by practically every newspaper in the land.

So it was the traditional grazing rights on Ben Lee which were at the heart of the Braes' crofters struggles. Lord Macdonald had decided to deprive them of the land so that it could be set aside for sport, and their considered request to have those rights restored was met with a curt refusal and a gratuitous insult. There followed the repulsing of the sheriff's officer, the pitch battle with fifty Glasgow policemen who had been imported to do what the sheriff's officer had failed to do, a tide of public sympathy which buoyed the crofters' struggles, the remarkable Royal Commission and the simple eloquence of the crofters' evidence which concluded with the words of their spokesman Angus Stewart.

'Give us land out of the plenty that is about. Give us land at a suitable rent.' The rot did not stop with the Braes folk, and in a sense it still has not stopped, but these days the crofting movement is professionally organised, has friends in high places up to and including the heir to the throne, and has forged links with conservation bodies like the RSPB and the John Muir Trust which even ten years ago would have sounded far-fetched fantasy. To echo Stewart, there is still plenty of land about that crofting might be given both on Skye and all across Gaeldom.

So there were two reasons why I was delving deep into the secret watercourse of the Allt an t-Sithein. One was because the burn's ever-deepening tunnel would bring me face to face with the inside of a small mountain, the rock heart at close, cold and clammy quarters. The other was because it is this of all mountains, this wide, blunt and bulky cornerstone of the Skye landscape beyond Sligachan, whose name became a monument to the day the rot first showed that it might not be unstoppable and that an apparently inexorable and odious tide could be turned.

It was cool in the heart of the gorge, the walls leaning close perhaps twice the width of the span of my arms. I slipped in one more pool and reached instinctively for the wall but it was plastered with a smooth and sodden lichenous gloss into which my fingertips dug and failed to hold. Instead I came away with a handful of spiders, three tiny brown mites, troglodyte creatures which could scarcely have anticipated this kind of disruption to their ordered lives. What had they to fear but the tumult of a spate and the haphazard passage of dipper and wren? I replaced the handful and hoped that my painstaking repair held good.

One last pool, waist deep and the colour of a rich old Talisker, and I was back on warming rock and making for the white light of the sun where the walls leaned back and widened and grew green again. That was enough gorge and I clambered high among heathers and rowans, and the head-high attentions of an aggressive female kestrel was as sweet as larksong.

The summit of Ben Lee was sensational, thickened with patches of alpine ladies mantle the size of carpet squares, scoured by the running-standing-sighing sprints of golden plover. Crossing the wide plateau was a procession from one territory into another, and the coy beauty of the birds (if anything so regally black and gold can be thought of as coy) was a constant companion. The flight call of adult males was everywhere on the air, and there are few sounds on the planet to which I would more gladly lend an ear, save perhaps a swan, a Sibelius symphony or a Stan Getz ballad. Not much else. To the east the foreground was all Raasay, the background a procession of mountains from Kintail to Suilven; and always at your back or over your shoulder the spreadeagle of the Cuillin grew ever wider and more handsome. Ravens were falling over themselves in the air, the young birds learning the flight skills of the adults and spilling thinly hysterical parodies of raven croaks as they fell and righted themselves and flew raggedly, crazily, happily. You almost expect to hear the birds giggle. Two golden eagles spun lazily down from the north and hunted low across the furthest edge of the plateau, but the ravens and the kestrels conspired to unsettle them. They took so much then soared contemptuously clear of their ragamuffin tormentors, up and up without a wing beat, then a right heel and a long high glide towards Raasay. I sat by the small summit cairn and watched them go until they were bird dust, then finally not even that. It would have been good to be an eagle making that flight on such a day.

I sat an hour by the cairn, thinking of Stewart and his contemporaries, thinking of the heaped straws of outrage which his people had borne for generations, scattering them miserably across the world, before this last straw was carelessly tossed onto the bowed back of their race, the right to graze beasts on Ben Lee. I judged this plover-loud cairn a better monument than the roadside cairn, but then thought better of the judgement. This is monument enough for Stewart and his people, but the roadside monument matters so that new generations – whether crofters or casually curious tourists – will pause and wonder and ask why. It should not be forgotten what happened here between Ben Lee and the waters of the Sound of Raasay, between the golden plovers and the red-throated divers, on behalf of the crofters of Gaeldom.

It was a long day, Friday the 26th of June, 1992, for I had first driven from Portree to the monument on the Braes Road, then on to the road end, then walked the shore of Loch Sligachan, then climbed the burn and dared the tunnel, then climbed Ben Lee, then dawdled among the plover and the alpine rugs, then returned to the car, then driven round Ben Lee to the camp site at Sligachan and pitched my tent. I retired to the Sligachan Hotel for food and drink, not precisely in that order, but I was lingering over another drink or two when I opened that day's copy of the West Highland Free Press (which explains why I can still remember the date). That paper is before me now as I write. Considering all that had preoccupied me through that day, my eyes leaped to the front page headline: 'Crofting estates are there for the taking'. I quote:

'A radical change in the interpretation of crofting law will deny landowners of their supposed right to half the development value of croft land and open the door to cheap and easy community ownership of crofting estates.'

'From now on crofters do not have to share with their landlord half the development value of croft land they sell to a third party. By nominating a designee who is not a member of their family the crofter simply has to pay 15 times the rent for the land he or she wishes to dispose of and can then force the landlord to transfer the title to the buyer of the land.'

'. . . the change follows a recent Court of Session appeal ruling reinforcing a decision of the Scottish Land Court which makes it clear that crofters do not have to share in the development value of croft land.'

'Importantly, the anomaly in the law opens the door to crofters to force the transfer of title of their crofts from their landlords to any nominee of their choice – effectively to change landlords if they so desire. The most obvious choice would be a company consisting of the crofters themselves.'

'The crofting world, and no doubt the land-owning class, will be stunned by the ruling which stands convention on its head. It seems that for years crofters have been making unnecessary payments to landlords for developing croft land.'

The concluding quote from Scottish Crofters Union director George Campbell had a fine historic ring about its last sentence:

'The opportunity now exists on problem estates for crofters to take affairs into their own hands. The landlords can become an irrelevance.'

In my quiet corner of the bar, I raised my glass to Angus Stewart.

Chapter Eleven

Many Nooked Bracadale

THE LIGHT has gone from the Island.

The township of Roag on its hill across the loch is a well-spaced string of lit squares. One flickers off near the shore, another lights up near the hillcrest and curtains close over it, dulling down its white glare. I can no longer see the shore or the township's hill or the higher ground behind, or the sawn-off mountain twins of Healabhal Mhor and Healabhal Bheag – MacLeod's Tables – which are such a landscape focal point of north-west Skye.

Many window squares stay black and unseen. Christmas and New Year will brighten and warm them briefly before the long winter darkness resumes. They bring their own shade of darkness after the blazing illusion of the festive season holidays. It will be Easter then before the illusion reappears and by then the Islanders will have butted their way head-down through the drabbest shades of winter, and the uneasy silent waiting darkness of the cold and unlit window squares is one more winter grievance in their midst.

Today I have watched the light fade through the early afternoon from another window which is not normally lit at this time of year either, for I have borrowed someone else's holiday cottage as a writing base, and as the wind stings small frenzies of white water all across Loch Bracadale's nooks, I ponder over my position. It is a south wind and a boisterous one, and Bracadale knows no defence against a south wind.

South winds have always blown uneasily on Skye shores. Many have borne north the holiday home owners whose windows are now black. In the process many houses have been pushed beyond the price Islanders can afford. There are Islanders living in caravans because they cannot afford to buy a house like this which is someone else's second home. Yet I can hardly deny that I am pleased to be here. The house is warm and dry and comfortable and the perfect base for a landscape writer who chooses to scour Skye through the worst of its winter weather and returns here soaked and frozen four days out of five in any one week. It belongs to friends of a friend and they live in the south of England. As soon as circumstances permit they plan to move here permanently. They have restored a traditional house and made a perfectly acceptable job of it. Yet in many people's eyes they are part of the problem rather than the solution, and because of what I am doing here and now, so am I.

For that reason as much as any other, I may never live on Skye, much as I think I would love to. The concept of 'belonging' is a precious one in Scotland, more so in the islands than other places. As the population of Skye has fallen so has that percentage of the population which is native. The Sound of Skye Gaelic, or Skye English for that matter, grows less familiar on the Island while the sound of mainland English is omnipresent. It is an elusive ideal that seeks to achieve that balance of native and incomer which would stabilise the uneasy compromise Skye has become. Change of land-ownership patterns may be part of it; positive discrimination in the sale of land and houses may be part of it; a Gaelic-led cultural revival may be part of it; greater political awareness of the realities of everyday life in such places may be part of it (Government interest in Skye is roused by controversy or tragedy and very little else). A Scottish Parliament, whether devolved or independent, cannot fail to do better, while the Skye Bridge furore is just one more example of the eccentric nature of Westminster Government at work in a corner of its jurisdiction which it likes to call 'remote'. If you live on Skye, there are few places more remote than Westminster.

But there is something else missing. Perhaps it is a sense of self-belief among the Skye people, the confidence to face the south wind head-on and devise shelter from it. It is a matter of the repair of a broken spirit. So much has been lost over so many years, notably so much lifeblood. What remains is perilously poised.

I gaze moodily out over the afternoon. Not for the first time in my life I am held in a snare which is Skye, loving it and grieving for it and caring so passionately for it, yet continually questioning my right to do any of these things. There are days and moods when I tell myself I have no right to pronounce on the place, yet seeing what I see and feeling what I feel, there are days when I tell myself I have no right not to. As always, the urge of the writer to write has the final say.

The water stirs again in a way which is not a stirring of the wind. The afternoon has been all gray's shades in which the scarlet accessories of vagabonding oystercatchers were too violent a shade. On the other hand, the herons which criss-crossed the head of Pool Roag in short, saggy flights were appropriately gray enough to be broken fragments of the day's Island. At the tide's lowest ebb there were seven in a hundred yards of shoreline, spaced regular as fence posts, waiting. The tide begins to flow, and as the new movement of water begins to swirl sluggishly I put the sounds in my mind of its sucking at the shoreline rocks, slapping petulantly at the muddy ooze where the herons stand; cold, fretful, winter-gray sea.

I speak aloud to no-one: 'Skye, what are you doing to me?' Then I wonder how many people over how many centuries have framed a variation of the same question in their own tongues. For the bottom line of Skye's unsolvable question is that it bewitches with its beauties, that the fickleness of its beauties only compounds the bewitching, and that it is quite unselective about those it bewitches. Otta Swire wrote it as well as anyone:

'Skye is a strange island in many ways. Those who visit it, whether from choice or by birth, either hate it wholeheartedly or else love it so dearly that they remain homesick for it until they die.'

I recognise myself among the latter, and there is nothing I can do about it. If I ever met the owners of this cottage, doubtless I would recognise the same homesickness in them, and in their affliction they would be just as helpless. Yet how I rage with the Islanders at the spectre of the black windows.

The water about the seaweed-sleek rocks is the colour of herons. As dusk gate-crashes mid-afternoon the herons fly and in their flight they are the colour of the dusk. They screech and they are the voice of the wind. For a while, at about 3.30pm, the white walls of Roag's cottages seem to intensify their whiteness. Day starts to rush from the land as though a second tide, a tide of light, had suddenly embarked on its fastest ebb. More squares light up on Roag's hill, and if there are window watchers up there they may see my window aglow in Vatten and mark the unaccustomed event, for isn't that window usually black until the holiday? The lit squares grow vivid, the white walls pale and fade and vanish, the high ground slips from discernible focus and Healabhal Mhor wears a shroud the shade of the dusk herons. The hill is cordoned off at the waist, and even its gray-black bulk is vanishing.

What is it like to be on Healabhal Mhor now, cold and sodden and sightless, and swathed in all that airy heron-shaded gray? I have climbed the Tables in all their shades over all my Skye years and I know. I know the dizzying, disconcerting, disorientating void of those plateau summits when there is no plateau to see, no Minch, no Cuillin, only the next gray yard and the previous one. With luck you find the summit cairn by bumping into it. Is that ice welded into the cairn's fissures? You draw breath in the lee of the cairn, swallow coffee which emerges hot from the flask but cools faster than you can drink it. You curse your silly addiction to such places. There are no comforting lit squares to hasten and hearten your descent on such a hilltop in its heron-dusk. But you stand again to face the wind's brunt and taste the Minch on it and you know no wind which tastes better. You feel as elemental as the wind and the Minch and you know no sensation which feels better.

Then you turn to follow your compass hand to the edge. You throw your mind about the hill-top's wide and steep-sided plateau. Think: which edges are too steep? Memory trembles. You make your best guess, follow the compass and hope it beckons to a good edge. You drop into the heron-cloud.

There are no longer, more tentative minutes of any mountain or hillside anywhere than the heron-cloud, trying to second-guess the next gray yard of steep downslope, the next gray yard and the next. Then the smaller country emerges far below your feet and there are lit squares where the map in your head says they should be, and there is the loch drained of all colour, and any heron crossing it now is black and late to the roost.

That is what it is like to be on the furthest, uppermost edge of my window's view this ebbing December afternoon. Long after you are safe and warm again you can still taste the Minch-wind on your lips.

On my Bracadale nook, the south wind has eased to a tired string of sighs redolent of all December's weariness. A stillness inveigles its way through the rocks and lies flat on the water in the lee of Roag Island. Four windows put their reflections on that blackening water, four trembling ladders of light.

A car curves round the loch's shore and climbs the hill which is all there is to Roag, pushing its headlight beam before it. Three-quarters of the way up it stops and its lights go out. Almost at once a window flares nearby as if a small spark of the light of Skye life has transferred from car to cottage. An old and barely sustainable image, fogged about the edges, is suddenly aglow in my mind: a leerie – a gas lamplighter – on a street in Dundee, little more than a ghost from earliest childhood trapped in a dull cavern of memory for forty years and liberated now by someone driving home to a Skye croft and splashing a square flame of light into the quiet landscape. That night, I would dream weirdly about squares of black and light, a chequered Island, willing the lit squares to resist the swarming advance of the black ones, jerking myself awake before every last lit square was snuffed.

Chapter Twelve

A Moment Among Swans

THE RIVER NUDGES into the north-west corner of Loch Suardal, a small, shallow and reedy water. The river's left bank survives beyond the loch shore as a slim peninsula fifty yards long, so that there is the flowing water of the river to one side, the still water of the loch to the other. I found it drifted white by the snow birds, twenty whooper swans strung out down the spit and in the shallows just beyond it, dozing fitfully through one more winter storm. Nature does not make roosts for wild swans much better than this, sheltered from Dunvegan's sea loch and all its winds by a high bank, favoured with good feeding which for a swan means submerged weed, and with just enough of a watersheet to accommodate twenty swans when they all decide to take off at once, which is how a flock of whoopers takes off most of the time.

The single track road to nowhere-very-much wraps round the west side of the loch, climbing as it unravels, so that it is fully fifty feet above the swans at its nearest point to their roost, and there is just enough room to ease a small car into a good vantage point. I switched off the engine, opened the window and settled to await the impact of my arrival on the swans, but no swan stirred. One head out of twenty was raised watching me, but quite unmoved, quite unalarmed. Perhaps the birds were too storm-weary, or perhaps they were sure enough of that road's sparse out-of-season traffic to know that a car is only a problem when it decants a mammal. I watched awhile, imprinting certain attitudes among the folding of the swans into my mind, scribbling notes and sketches to assist the imprinting. I took a few photographs in appalling light, noted down the presence of two family groups, and was head down in my writing pad when the commotion began.

What I heard first was a solitary widgeon calling loudly, a shrill ricochet of sound like the second half of a wolf-whistle, and swimming fast downstream. Then it flew, and the reeds and hidden shallows fired salvoes of widgeon, mallard, goldeneye, perhaps a hundred-and-fifty spring-heeling into the air. I was about to follow them with the glasses across the loch when a heron burst in on the chaos, hot on the solitary widgeon's tail. The image of a hot heron in a winter rain on Skye is, I concede, a curious one, but this heron was bristling and hot. It came fast (for a heron) downriver, screaming, and more or less as the swimming widgeon became airborne and provoked the duck panic, the heron must have seen the swans. By now every head was periscope high, a straight line of twenty raised necks and swivelling heads. The heron made a pointed swerve and lunged at the first swan, causing it to duck in self-defence, then like one of these set-piece arrangements of dominoes you can topple by touching the first one, it flew down the line at swan-head-height so that every bird had to duck in turn. As the heron passed, each collapsed swan neck straightened again and each head uttered an astonished 'woop?'

Between first swan and last the heron rasped three oaths, and by way of adding insult to insult, swooped down on a tight raft of ducks and rasped two more.

I was still trying to make sense of the whole episode when I saw above the wood on the loch's far shore the ebony shape of a cruising eagle. That allowed me to compose a plausible theory which goes like this:

The heron had been fishing up-river when the eagle took a mischievous pot shot at it, for something to do on such a day (herons do not get on well with large birds of prey, especially eagles and buzzards and I have heard of an osprey forcing one down onto the surface of a loch). The swan sentry was watching me and missed the eagle. The others were dozing heads-in-spines and would have missed a flypast of eagles. The heron, startled and annoyed and doubtless fearful, headed flat-out downstream where the hapless solitary widgeon was feeding. The widgeon swam instinctively away from the heron but suddenly detected its malevolent pace, recognised itself as a sitting duck for the heron to torment, and flew, too fast and too agile for herons, even a hot heron. Then the heron saw the swans sitting up, convenient as a coconut shy, and vented its wrath by shying at every coconut. By the time the heron touched down across the loch, the eagle was half a mile away and heading for the clouds, and when I left a few minutes later, only one swan head was visible and I was grinning.

Chapter Thirteen

Waternish of the Wolves

WATERNISH BEGINS with Fairy Bridge. If you are among the lucky ones who live there you will say it ends with Fairy Bridge and that beyond lies Skye. Note 'Fairy Bridge' not 'the Fairy Bridge' or – heaven forbid – 'the fairy bridge'. A stranger's passing glance may see only an old stone bridge carrying a disused stretch of the road across a burn, but it is a *place*, not a thing. Somewhere near the far end of Waternish you will see a road sign. It says: 'Fairy Bridge 4'.

Waternish is of all Skye's wings, the one most out on a limb. Sleat boasts three ferry terminals, Duirinish is veined enough with roads for a stranger to need a road map, Trotternish has a ring road and Portree on the doorstep. But Waternish is a string of road between the crest of a long hill and the sea, beginning with Fairy Bridge and ending with a ruined church famed for a massacre and for the last resting place of an infamous madwoman. A few cul-de-sac diversions from the road do not mitigate Waternish's isolation.

There is something almost tangibly Norse at work here, something more of Shetland than Skye. It is not easy to pin down, but Waternish is more wind-scrubbed than most places on Skye, and Skye communities are rarely so four-square to the sea as this. That and a network of well-made and well-maintained drystane dykes and the untypical purpose-built fishing village of Stein.

There is a clutch of Norse-tongued names all across the peninsula too – Lusta, Halistra, Dun Hallin, Trumpan, the offshore islands of Isay, Mingay and Clett. Waternish is its own island with a land bridge to Skye, like Ardnamurchan's purely physical attachment to mainland Scotland.

All this makes for self-containment in a community. Some Islanders look askance at the Waternish folk, and doubtless it happens in reverse too, but when did the Gael not look askance at those who live at the extremities of Gaeldom? The landscape of Waternish is a factor in all this too, for in terms of its raw beauty and especially its seaward prospects, there is nothing like it, even on Skye.

So it all begins at Fairy Bridge, and that is flanked by bad omens, but then it always was. A Fairy Bridge at a crossroads was always destined to be an unchancy place. But the bridge where unexplained murders happened and horses shied away or crossed fearfully and ghosts discouraged travellers is now a good viewpoint for one more of Skye's too numerous forestry plantations and that gruesome line of Western Isles pylons. Worst of all unless you are a horse, the newest realignment of the old crossroads bypasses the bridge and consigns it to the ignominy of a tourist curio. Still, not a few Skye folk who know better will wave to the Fairies of Fairy Bridge when they pass by as they used to wave when they had to cross, to appease whatever spirits must be appeased there. It is just too hard now to tune into those older eras when folklore was still a stitch in the weave of everyday life, when a stone bridge could instil real fear into the minds of those who crossed it. We are beyond it all now, most of us, we who have the sophistication and the technology and the contempt for landscape to hurl forty miles of cable on pylons from Broadford to Ardmore Point on Waternish, then sling it across the Minch to brighten the street lights in Stornoway or a TV picture in Benbecula. In such circumstances, what chance has a stone bridge, and not even the Fairies of Fairy Bridge can resist such an overwhelming progress. But if you want to furrow the brows of one or two of the oldest Skye folk just scoff away at the top of your voice about Fairy Bridge and the nonsense of its ghosts and its murders and its queasy horses, and see the black looks you will get. The longest living memories will tell you of the time when it was otherwise, when this wing of Skye was well guarded by the spirits of Fairy Bridge, when there was more to it all than a predatory gleam in the eye of some academic folklorist.

Otta Swire was a Skye woman from an old Skye family. She learned her folklore by word of mouth, from her mother who heard it in turn from a great aunt born in 1799. Where it had meandered, and whose mouths might have uttered it before is anyone's guess. When Otta Swire set about writing the stories down, she did so for her own children, and from the unique perspective of one who is of the very folklore itself. The resulting book, *Skye – The Island and Its Legends*, was the first book about Skye I ever bought and I never tire of it.

It is not an old book (first edition 1961), but it carries the authentic ring of the centuries, and although she writes with much good humour and a leavening of light scepticism, she draws breath here and there to give the unexplainable a chance to sink in for the benefit of the unconverted. One such pause for thought is at Fairy Bridge, where she tells this story:

> My grandfather, John Robertson of Orbost, was much puzzled by the shying of every horse at the bridge, whether driven, ridden or led across. He himself, an experienced horseman and no believer in either ghosts or fairies, had just the same trouble with his horses as did those who feared the place. He believed that a rider or a driver, himself nervous at the bridge, would convey his fear to his horse, causing it to shy, and that the beast did

not forget and would always afterwards shy at its own remembered panic. One day he bought a new horse from Ireland. It came by sea to Dunvegan and so had not to cross Fairy Bridge. At that time, too, he had a friend from the south staying with him who had never before been in Skye and knew neither Skye geography nor Skye stories. This friend offered to try the new horse and my grandfather, seeing the chance of testing his theory, gave him directions for a ride which involved crossing Fairy Bridge twice. When the rider returned he was eagerly questioned about the horse. A good beast, he pronounced her, good tempered, steady and pleasant to ride, but evidently nervous of water as she had shied twice, both times while crossing a bridge. Curiously, too, it was the same bridge both times and she took no notice of the others they had crossed. Needless to add, it was Fairy Bridge.

The road across Fairy Bridge now is cracked and growing green. A slick of new tarmac slopes down from the realigned road but stops well short of the bridge, just enough to lure a tourist car down to the hideous tourist-blue information board on its pole. (Tourist-blue is that shade which the manufacturers of bad postcards used to use for the sea and the sky in the Highlands, and now that it has largely disappeared, the colour has been adopted by the Scottish Tourist Board which would rather you didn't know the colour gray exists in places like Skye.) A new forestry plantation, the corner of a monstrous sprawl of ten million trees between here and Edinbane, is a landscape glower. A gravel and grit store for Highland Regional Council's roads department defaces the crossroads. It is a curious place these days to invite a tourist to stop, and whatever miseries the spirits of Fairy Bridge may have inflicted on earlier eras, the late twentieth century has inflicted its own copious revenge on the place.

Legend and historical fact (where the latter can be separated from the former – never an easy task among Gaels) have given Waternish a bad press. Every legend is liberally bloodied, witches performed black deeds in the guise of cats, the Macdonald feud commemorated at Trumpan was gruesome even by their own dire standards, and the peninsula has the reputation of being the last Skye stronghold of wolves. Whether this last fact accounts for much of the darker side of Waternish lore is nothing more than a speculation of my own. Certainly, for all the cultural sophistication of the Gaels, they suffered from the same blind prejudice towards wolves as most other peoples in most other countries of the wolf's world. The wolf was undoubtedly a harrier of man's stock, but not of man. The wolf is a defensive pacifist, and the Little Red Riding Hood syndrome is not just a fairy story, it is a lie. That the Gael swallowed it whole and gleefully exterminated the wolf from his realm makes him no different, no more and no less culpable in the crime of wolf extinction than the rest of Scots, Britons, and half the tribes of the planet.

So at least one Waternish legend may have a factual basis to it. It is that wolves were bothersome enough hereabouts for the natives to have built wolf traps, and that a hunter who fell into one such trap was only saved by a friend who caught a trapped wolf by the tail and held it until the man scrambled free. Typical wolf behaviour in such a situation (discounting the unlikely tail-holding fantasy) would have been to back away and leave the man to his fearful escape, although I applaud the natural justice of the hunter succumbing to his quarry trapped in his own wretched pit, even though it wouldn't have happened that way.

It is a sketchy tradition, undocumented and undated, although it cannot be much more recent than the end of the seventeenth century, by which time Scotland's wolves were staring extinction in the face. Seton Gordon wrote in the 1920s that 'the wolf pits are on the hill near Trumpan and must be of a great age, for the oldest inhabitant has no tradition of when the last wolf was trapped in Skye.' Still, if the wolves were to cling on anywhere in the islands, Waternish is as likely a place as any, especially as it would have been a well-wooded place three hundred years ago. The coastal woods under Geary and the tumultuous alders which shroud Waternish House show that trees are a convivial enough part of the natural order of things when circumstances don't conspire against them. You see it too across Loch Bay where a conifer plantation stops, the cliff belt about the waist of Sgurr a'Bhagh begins, and beneath it hang folds of skirts fashioned from native trees, untrampled, ungrazed, unfelled, unburned, the natural order. Watch it light up a quiet autumn afternoon and know the difference. The wolves would have loved it.

Two hours of usable daylight, no prospect of afterglow or moonlight to steal from the midwinter night, merely the certainty of a dirty afternoon a week before the shortest day, and growing progressively dirtier. Wind had blasted rain into submission, but that was all that had submitted. It had looked an unenticing prospect when the squalls thudded through a half-dark noon, but by one o'clock they had ceased their percussive flaying of my window and I rose from the writing table to go out into the Island. By two I was scrambling through a little gully on the flank of Beinn na Boineide and the air was the icy breath of the Arctic oceans.

I have long since learned to value the fragments stolen from the unlikeliest of days, long since learned to value the discipline of making the effort to go when the word-logged brain demands rest. Two hours on a hillside in Waternish is an energising expedition. Senses dulled by too long a stint at the typewriter are galvanised by release. A brain crammed with tired words is blown clean and uncluttered and goes eagerly with the wolf or follows a buzzard on some flight of fancy. I snatch at ideas, light, atmosphere, smell, sound, brief encounters with landscape and wildlife. Perhaps there will be a glimpse of that still elusive will-o-the-wisp, the heart of Skye?

There is no time for the long patient stalk, no need for a pack, no preparation. There is just the going and the being there and the slow unwinding to the rhythm of the wilds. I love the hour just before the darkening, whatever the season, the fading away of the day and the day creatures, the unfolding of night lives, the brief hour of overlapping regimes. In a land like this, an owl might confront an eagle, the turning head of a hanging buzzard will follow with one eye a skein of whoopers homing in on a roosting loch. At the same hour, a fox might once have stepped deferentially aside from a hunting wolf.

At a little over 1,000 feet, Beinn na Boineide is the summit of all Waternish. The wind was a moan in the pylon wires, and two pylons with extra embellishments were spitting high voltage abuse. I passed under them as tentatively as a horse crossing Fairy Bridge. The presence of the wires here is, if anything, more loathsome than at Loch Sligachan, and they endear themselves to no-one with a series of notices along the roadside which celebrate the achievement of what they euphemistically call 'The Western Isles Connection'.

I tramped out of the gorge and put a high and wide shelf of Beinn na Boineide's moorland slopes between me and the 'Connection', disconnecting myself as it were, and breathing easier as the sea widened and Waternish's own shape and shade of winter moorland hill lengthened. With no light in the sky the moor grasses smouldered with their own dark flame, and my eyes found the brightest shade in the landscape by looking down. The cloud cover had lowered now, enough to camp on Waternish's crest, so I walked north keeping below it, following the line of ancient overgrown dykes, stumbling on the spoor of an old track long reclaimed by the moor. Once I might have walked here among hazel, oak, birch, alder, aspen, a high and airy scrub of woodland; once I could have stood among such trees and watched a wolf catch my scent on the wind and step quietly away from it: I tried to imprint such a scene on today's landscape but a real life buzzard gave voice yards away, wrecking the fantasy, but replacing it with one of nature's unextinct fascinations instead. I crouched low and still for I was behind and above the bird and well placed to watch as she worked the wind. When I locked the glasses on to her she almost filled them. Strictly speaking she was hovering, but not in the way that a kestrel hovers. The kestrel's technique is to fly into the wind at the wind's speed, flicker-winged, fan-tailed. The buzzard rather sits on the wind, wings held in a rigid concave, flexing them only for the smallest of adjustments, or to drift away a yard or two over the moor, to turn into the wind again, legs down like an undercarriage, but for all the stillness of her body, her head is a restless workaholic, scanning below, scanning ahead, scanning to either side, and scanning the far horizons.

For perhaps five minutes I watched the buzzard from my higher vantage point, during which time she was never further than twenty yards from the position where I had first seen her. At last she drifted towards me, sideways and slightly backwards, letting the wind do the work. As the bird drifted, she also rose, climbing the hillside backwards. In that attitude she passed above my head, low and vast, and the tables were instantly turned. For as long as I resisted the temptation to look up to see what was going on, the buzzard appeared to take my hooded and moor-coloured stillness at face value, drifting onwards and upwards and sideways and backwards, but from the moment she passed above and behind my head I was caught in a disconcerting no-man's land. To move was to betray myself.

She would be trying now to make sense of my crouching unfamiliar shape in her territory where every rock and bog made an intimate network of landmarks. That thorough, head-swivelling, wind-fingering scrutiny of wildest Waternish which I had so admired until moments ago was now riveted – I could sense it – on me, the watcher watched. So I studied my own self-imposed immobility. How an absence of movement sharpens all the senses! I became suddenly and intensely aware of everything I could see without moving. A lizard, looking ancient, flickered over a bare patch among the heather; a black and gray boat emerged from a hidden shore; a horse kicked the air on a croft and a kestrel crossed its field, fast downwind; the boat pirouetted in a bay and stopped; a vivid red-orange spider the size of a small button crossed the lizard's patch of bare earth. Where was the buzzard now?

I threw every effort into listening, but the wind was a thudding wail which my ears could not shut out and nothing else carried through. I began to move my head slowly to the left and right, buzzard-style, searching sweeps of all the land and sky that came into view. Nothing, but that still left all Waternish above and behind me at the bird's disposal. I pushed my head right back and stared at the sky above, the empty sky above. Yet I still sensed the bird close by.

The wind thumped into me and bit cold and deep and my un-buzzard-like tolerances gave in to the pounding. I stood up stiffly and turned and found the buzzard a dozen yards away, above and behind, regarding me side-headed, close enough for me to see the orange of her eye, and how the awesomeness of the bird's presence magnifies from below! If there are rabbits on Waternish, I feel for them!

The buzzard hung a moment longer, then a shimmy and a dipped wing and a raising and lowering of her undercarriage took her to a new stance on the wind below and ahead of me again, so that I was once more looking down on the length of her back and tail and the dark spread of her upper wings. We might have been old foes sizing each other up, so utterly did the world shrink suddenly to exclude everything other than the two of us and the moorland shelf where we watched each other, all pretence abandoned.

She was Macdonald, I Macleod, sometimes the other way round, and we jousted for possession of a circle of the wide world. I held the moorland shelf, she the air above and below, and still she would not drift further than a few yards. After long minutes of this, I began to wonder if the thing would be resolved before darkness engulfed us an hour hence, but the buzzard abruptly abandoned her airy perch, thrust forward both vivid yellow legs, threw high both wings, landed twenty yards away, dipped her head into a small hollow and raised it again bloodied.

All was prosaically explained. I had put the bird up from a sheep carcass when she first drew herself to my attention. She had lingered not to be a symbolic clan chieftain but to establish whether or not I posed a threat to her meal. Having satisfied herself that I didn't have what it takes to sunder rotting sheep flesh, she returned to her meal, still watching.

So I backed off then to a higher rock where I could watch for a while and leave the buzzard in peace. Sure enough, the rock revealed the carcass in what was no more than a depression in the heather. Not a sheep carcass, though, a fox. When I left half an hour later to walk down to the road in the murky half-light, the wind had eased, the Minch was a wan and eerie green, and (like so many Macdonald galleys) a flotilla of tightly disciplined showers was about to flay the shore somewhere up about Trumpan.

Trumpan is irresistible Skye. The ruinous church is high on a headland of the Minch, so boisterous winds are more or less compulsory. Some of the coldest sunlight I have ever seen shone here. The churchyard itself would not be out of place in Strath (which now seems a world away, such are the rarefied and introverting elements of Waternish) with its pagan relics co-operating with Christian graves of many centuries, a peaceable enough fellowship in old stone whatever their old warring differences in the flesh. There was peace here too for the bones of Lady Grange, infamous madwoman subjected to piteous incarceration on St Kilda. One more stone confirms her last resting place.

But Trumpan is also a monument to a massacre, perhaps – but only perhaps – the most infamous of all the confrontations between Macdonald and Macleod, and the one Macdonalds least like to be reminded of when they celebrate still the outrage of the Massacre of Glencoe. Then they were the victims, but at Trumpan they set fire to the thatched church during a Sabbath service. Those of the congregation who escaped the fire perished unarmed on Macdonald swordpoints.

The motive, of course, like the motive for so many episodes of clan warfare, was revenge, in this case the massacre of two hundred Macdonalds by Macleods in a cave on Eigg, though why Trumpan was seized on to repay that bloody debt is not revealed. Accounts of the massacre of Trumpan are typically inconsistent, and as the story has been regurgitated continually over four hundred years, it is small wonder that it varies according to the source. The common ground appears to be this:

The Macdonalds landed in galleys mysteriously undetected by the sentries on the tower of Dunvegan Castle who later saw only the flames of the burning church and raised a belated alarm. The Macdonalds fired the church and all but one of the congregation died at once in the fire or by the sword. The one was an old woman who squeezed through a window, and though dying, survived long enough to find a child who ran to raise the alarm elsewhere on Waternish.

The Macleods mustered what strength they could, which was little enough, and battle was joined below Trumpan on Ardmore

Point. The Macdonalds were a substantial and select fighting force, the Macleods a hasty and inadequate gathering, and there should have been only one outcome, but here the story slips into its most celebrated controversy. The Fairy Flag was waved!

The Fairy Flag is probably the most famous rag in the world. It was to be waved when Clan Macleod confronted crisis, but only three times. It was only ever waved twice, and according to one branch of the legend this was one of the occasions. Others say no, that was the Battle of Waternish not long before, and between the same enemies. Whether it was waved or furled, it seems the Macleods' numbers suddenly grew to a great host and the Macdonalds took to their heels and headed for the galleys, at which point the story takes its least plausible turn. It seems that the Macdonald galleys had been left high and dry by the receding tide and with their retreat cut off they were slaughtered on the shore, selling their lives dearly in the process. But these were the sons of the Lords of the Isles, master seamen as well as master warriors. For centuries they roved the western waters and the Hebrides, thriving among some of the trickiest waters anywhere. Would they really have been so careless as to permit retreat to be thwarted by the tide of all things? It is hardly likely.

Still, there was a massacre, and there was a battle, and they heaped the bodies into the shadow of a dyke at Ardmore and tipped the stones over on top of them, and called it with a nice touch of Gaelic irony, Blar Milleadh Garaidh, the Battle of the Spoiling of the Dyke. If like me you don't know what to believe, visit Dunvegan Castle and stand in front of the Fairy Flag and wonder. It may not clarify events on this troubled shore, but it will teach you perhaps that history is nowhere more elusive than on Skye, that from time to time there have been elements at work in the shaping of the Island's destiny which defy logic and military historians and are best left where they lie. Like the mystery of Fairy Bridge, we have put too much distance and too much deafness between ourselves and the old ones who would cross fearfully. Too much scepticism and too much worthy research have deadened the wavelengths which once sang between a people and a flag, their ears and the pad of a Waternish wolf.

Chapter Fourteen

The Fantastic Highway

IT BEGINS more or less where Portree ends (where it creeps northward into something fearfully like a suburb), a climbing crag above Dun Gerashader on the Staffin road. The first rock of many miles of rock is Creag an Fhitich which is the Crag of the Raven. It ends sixteen miles to the north in a massively hacked and fractured slab-sided prow sweeping down to a high moorland only a mile-and-a-bit from the Island's northmost shore. Throughout its length you are rarely out of sight or earshot of crags and ravens.

It is a fantastic highway, this spinal cord of Trotternish, flirting with the 2,000 feet contour for many of its miles. The very frontiers of Gaeldom range along your horizons, the Western Isles to the west, the mountain-crazed seaboard of the north-west Highlands to the east. The Trotternish Ridge is Skye's overworld, an eagle realm inevitably, swooping, tilting, broad-backed, the mightiest wing of the Skye bird. Its summits may not be things of Cuillin fame and spectacle, but if you were to thread them all in a single journey you would march up against great sheets of skies, hung walls of skies founded in great sheets of seas. Watch a Sutherland-bound squall skip across twenty miles of northern ocean, followed by skeins of squalls homing in like geese, but soundless.

It is a long, tortuous and relentless highway too, and if you tread its crest you must also accept that you will miss out on its greatest claim to fame, for that struts its spectacle below your feet. You may climb any one of the Trotternish summits by way of a gentle walk up from the west, quiet unsung ways like Glen Uig. But the eastern flank – if you travel below it rather than above it – begins to unfold ever more preposterous variations on that craggy theme you first encountered under Creag an Fhitich. That long single mountain which is the bulk of Trotternish has broken apart all along this eastern flank and piece by piece it slips (at geology's own unfathomable pace) towards the sea. It is not as if the Old Man of Storr is abseiling down his mountainside and will stop the traffic while he crosses the road: rather it is that his millimetric advance will one day (not soon, not soon) slip a millimetre too many and he will fall flat on his multi-million-year-old face.

But the Old Man and his rock pinnacle cronies are out-Storred by a yet more illustrious gathering a few miles to the north. That grand old maestro among mountain photographers, W A Poucher, was no writer, but in a page of text preceding his photographs of the Quiraing in his classic *The Magic of Skye*, he offered up this:

> The weird rocks of Quiraing make the most bizarre landscape in Britain . . . On two occasions I ascended to the Table which is secretly hidden high up amid the gaunt, grotesque pinnacles of Quiraing. The first time I got wet to the skin and saw nothing of its amazing rock architecture, but nevertheless witnessed one of those demonstrations of

the 'Wrath of the Gods' when all elements combine to transform a masterpiece of nature into a wild cauldron of the Devil . . .

It is not an uncommon experience among Quiraing addicts, nor are analogies with the Devil, for on the wrong day it can be a hellish black hole. Poucher's masterly series of photographs were taken on a subsequent occasion of 'sailing white clouds, blue sky and brilliant sunlight' and appeared so often in so many publications that they defined the Quiraing in the minds of countless admirers who subsequently beat a path up past the Needle (an astounding free-standing 120-foot obelisk which signposts the way into the Quiraing's inner Sanctuary which in turn guards the Table) and met the Devil head on. I have a Devil-day of my own, which I compounded with a certain primitive folly.

The first mistake was to climb at all, for the mountain was a sodden, gritty mess with no reliable hand-and-foot-hold from top to bottom. The second was to eschew the messy and hideously eroded path up past the Needle and opt for a long steep gully which started innocuously enough and quickly lost patience with this fool on his fool's errand. Conditions worsened as the gully climbed and steepened, the rain bore down almost like a burden, and the clouds bore down with it. I was quickly engulfed. For as long as I was obviously able to retrace my steps back down the gully should things become impassable, I was comfortable enough, but once I had slithered up over a rough conglomeration of rock and loose rubble I suddenly removed that option at a single thoughtless stroke and was compelled to climb on. Progress became a slow and steepening farce, the rock running with water, the mountainside between the rocks turning to mud which smeared onto the rock with every footstep, and not a few handholds. I heard my own voice, sounding ominously distant, mutter, 'I don't like this', and half an hour later and not much higher up the gully, I heard myself say it again. I rounded on myself angrily: 'If you don't like it, what the bloody hell are you doing here? Get on with it!' I put three fast movements together and was over an obstacle which I had been studying fearfully for ten minutes.

I told myself: 'Get over that next outcrop and you can walk to the top,' and from where I stood I believed it. I climbed the last fifty feet on raw adrenalin, an unhealthy brew in its undiluted state, and when I lipped over the rim of the gully and saw that I had breached the Sanctuary walls and faced nothing more than a grassy stroll to the Table, I shouted an unseemly greeting – part glee, part relief – to the empty arena. It is a staggering place to be, especially after such an entry, and with the rain cloud hovering up and down the rock walls and stacks and pinnacles of the arena, so that the whole mountain mass seemed to swim and darken and lighten and tremble.

Then I heard a familiar voice, a flutey song so out of place in this gargantuan setting that at first I could not identify the singer. Then a small shape detached itself from a crevice twenty feet above my head and perched on a boulder six feet away, where it sang again: a robin. Skye has a pointed way of putting you in your place.

I ate lunch on the Table, although my exploits in the gully made it wet and late by about two hours. The rain stopped, the cloud thickened, and I sat in a shroud. Two sounds penetrated: the fall of a burn down the cliff at my back and the short, staccato and gruff whoops of two ravens. I kept walking into the centre of the Table and turning – sunwise – watching the pattern of the broken rock mass as I turned. The table is a raised grassy sward, a hundred yards long and not quite as wide, standing proud from the mountain mass and quite surrounded by inconceivable rock shapes. The stacks which rear from the mountainside many feet below the level of the Table seem to peer across its surface at you, Mad Hatters to your Alice, though why Alice should be sitting in the middle of the Table . . . oh, such places have a way of unhinging your thought processes.

I left Alice where I found her and wandered along the base of the rearing cliff. Up on the Fantastic Highway today, peering over the lip of this same cliff, there would be nothing of this, just a swirl of gray in a Devil's Cauldron. Uncoiled springs of roseroot leaped up from improbable cracks in the cliff-face, and the walls thickened with splashes of moss campion and saxifrages and other alpines. I had not expected a garden, any more than I had expected a robin.

I descended by the way I should have climbed, and won the prizes of confronting the Needle for the first time from above and out at me from a chrysalis of smoky cloud.

Leafing through Poucher's photographs now, I smile at period-piece captions like 'I scan the gigantic precipices' and 'Grim guardians of the mystic sanctuary', but he had an unerring touch among mountains and *The Magic of Skye* has some of his best work. I finger his gigantic precipices and I feel the grit under my fingernails, smell the mountain, taste the fear. Poucher died a few years ago in his mid-nineties. I met him once, when he was ninety, and doing a promotional tour for a new book of Highland photographs. He had photographed mountains all over the world, but at my mention of his book *The Magic of Skye*, his face lit. 'Skye,' he said, 'is my favourite.' Why? 'The light.' He thought a few moments, then said:

'I have a gift. I take no credit for it. I was born with it. Given today's standard of equipment, anyone can take competent, technically correct photographs. Whether they can make good pictures?' and his mouth closed in a thin line, the stooped shoulders shrugged, the white palms upturned, the gesture of finality from one who had nothing to prove. There is a modern pocket-sized edition of *The Magic of Skye* and I urge you to have nothing to do with it: seek out instead a good copy of the A4-sized original. A first edition might cost you £50 now, but it's the one he would like you to judge him by.

Perhaps one day I will have a glittering blue day on the Table, but I am in no hurry to climb again. What with my Devil day and his photographs, between us we make good pictures.

Chapter Fifteen

The Heart of Skye

The Heart of Skye
is a moor, not a mountain,
wind-washed, bone bare.

Here kindling was hewn
for all hearths,
keen-scent smokes
adrift, kin-mingling,
born back moorwards
to hew, to blaze again.

Like all hearts
the moor is unlovely
but loyal, pure
pulse-purveyor of life
till near death.

So why falter now?
Be still, hear
how it beats out
of your time!

The Island hews
mainland kindling
(the heart is by-passed);
draws water
from mainland wells
(the moor-spring sweetness
wastes on the sea);
forges shackles
from mainland bridges
(listen: the boatyard is still).

The Heart of Skye
is a flame, barely burning.
Feel the chill round the hearth!

IF YOU LOOK at a small-scale map of Skye, one small enough to show only the Island silhouette and the line of the main roads, the shape of a ghost mushrooms north and west up out of Sligachan, bounded by Portree and Dunvegan and the sea lochs of Snizort Beag and Greshornish. Somewhere about the waist of the ghost (if anything as amorphous as a ghost can be deemed to have a waist) a slip of a road sets out from Bracadale, creeps up a gorge, crosses the high moorland watershed, and dumps its travellers unceremoniously at Portree's unflattering back door. Either side of that road is wide open Skye, miles of it, and you can even shut the sea briefly from your mind.

It is a land on no-one's list of favourite Skye landscapes. Poucher never lingered here to make good pictures. For once the landscape is not instantly definable as Skye. Yet always there are glimpses: a far Cuillin through a cleft, a glitter of Loch Bracadale from a crest of the road, a clutch of Portree rooftops; and always from the highest ground there are more Cuillin, MacLeod's Tables, Beinn Tianavaig – Portree's personal Schiehallion. But there it is the moor's unexpected scope which imposes. On Skye where mountains seem to be forever fending off the sea, the surprise is that there is so much room. Here and there the moor rises in shallow, angular tiers to small flat and round summits with names like 'Cruachan' which is more or less 'Lump', which in turn is more or less appropriate. It is a lumpy moor.

I think of the place on a day of late autumn. The summer birds have gathered and gone, but at the summit of the road enigmatically called Leacan Nighean an t-Soisalaich – the Gravestone of the Daughter of the Chisolm – a single curlew crosses my path, stalking out from the roadside verge, perfect silhouette crossing the road precisely along the crest with only the sky for a backcloth. But at the sight of me the bird lifts, a dangling curve, and instantly there are three more in its wake, each its black mirror image, then at a blink there is a loose flock of fifteen low over the moor and restored to their familiar gray and brown as they put land behind them. They drift against the wind on still wings, alight on a green shelf. The flight is slow and weary, the flock listless, rising again within seconds. Again and again over the next few days I would encounter the flock between here and Bracadale, rarely still, the restlessness of migration's urges still on their wings, and whether they were urged on or stayed the winter I never knew for our meetings were curtailed by a migration of my own to Sleat. But for a few days we roved the moor, the curlews and I, always meeting more than once each day, always their signature a far or a near gathering of downward curves – backs-and-tails, heads-and-bills, unbeating wings – and always soundless.

I have walked up from Bracadale putting the moorland garb on slowly. Sometimes it is too easy and too thoughtless to whip up from the coast by car and step out on the summit, the transition too fast, too remote if the day's purpose is to watch the landscape. So I walk a long and toilsome hour and I have already immersed in the moorland mood by the time I encounter the first curlew silhouette. I have watched the moor emerge and widen, seen Bracadale recede, watched old birch woods of the sheltered places, climbed to that elemental watershed on the widest back of the Island, then on up onto the small summit of Am Maol where a huge sky is put at my disposal.

The morning's feeble sunshine is being ruthlessly extinguished by the crawling progress over hours of a weather front. There is no rain, at least not yet, just an eerie smothering of colour and visibility. It is as if a steel helmet is being clamped down on the Island. I choose a rock which cuts out the wind but still gives me a wide arc of moorland to watch. To the north the moor vanishes in the all-consuming advance of the grayness, but to the south-east colour still lingers, soft tones of all autumn's shades, what Gavin Maxwell called Skye's 'plum-red distance'. Hazy sunlight can strike no hard edges there, and pin down no deep shadow, but the muted riches of the colours weave a fetching garb and the moor looks well in it. In the north I see the colour fade and fade by slow degrees, waning as the gray advances and waxes ineloquent. Between the stronghold of colour and the citadel of gray, the progression across the landscape from one to the other is like a photographer's test strip which never quite gets the exposure right.

Within all that light and shade the moor is a deep brown constant, burnished with the flaming insinuations of late-autumn-contemplating-winter, but it halts abruptly at the one straight line in the landscape. It is the boundary of green croft land.

You look at crofts like these from a high outpost of a moor like this and you marvel. They were hewn from the worst of the land and by relentless re-working of the same patch and the fertilising effect of a few beasts for many generations, each generation inheriting a marginally improved land. In that way, crofting has literally created its own soil. Land capable of sustaining agriculture of a kind has been contrived from land which was once palpably incapable. At its best, it is a good environment for people and wildlife, and the arguments for its thoughtful expansion are irresistibly persuasive commonsense, which doubtless explains why governments have ignored them and their wisdom, creating instead a climate which encourages the landscape vandalism of grotesquely overdone plantation forestry which now encroaches massively on this moor. The economics of such forestry here are nonsense, the job security derisory, the smothering of landscape and wildlife and crofting opportunity catastrophic. The ancient lineage of the moor, the old lineage of the people are abruptly severed with no prospect of repair. The moor and the croft are interchangeable: a derelict croft can become moor again, or it can be reclaimed and become croft again, and new crofts can always subtly infiltrate the moor. But the new forests wreck the moor and deny the crofter. Henceforth the forested land will grow only poor trees for mainland pulp. It is not a fitting climax to an Island tradition. One more mainland regime has been thoughtlessly imposed on the Island and for all the protests from within the Island and from further afield (for the Skye landscape has many distant admirers), it goes on still.

All over the Island the trees evoke resentment. Oldest memories remember oak and birchwoods. Who plants one now? For that matter, who throws a fence round the fragmentary old woods which still cling on to let them save their own wild lives?

The same memories recall more people on the moor. Hearths were sustained by its peat, and stoical communities lived out in its raw embrace. A few still do, hidden places like Glenmore strung out along a small road and clawing another acre of green from the brown. Such places are nothing less than the vertebrae of the Island's backbone, and without the strength of the crofting townships, the heart of Skye is a doomed pulse.

How this moor must have changed! The wolves which lingered

longest on Waternish must once have revelled in its light and open woods, keeping the company of other creatures long consigned to their ultimate fate of museum pieces. Duns and souterrains and other stone relics betray a long human presence. Who knows now what feet, forbye wolves', might have trekked the line of the moorland road I have just followed, forging links perhaps out from Bracadale's brochs and cairns to Borve's brochs and standing stones or the forts north of Portree. Who now could comprehend their fears and aspirations? And what might they have made of Skye's aspirations now? And what might we still learn from them, in particular from their closeness to the land, their co-operation with nature?

The trouble with posing such questions is that while the tribal ancients would have yoked their own ambitions to the constraints of nature, in today's Island the voice of nature is a barely audible cry on the wind, and the concept of 'the constraints of nature' is quite extinct. Nature can no longer exercise constraints.

Take the question of the Skye bridge. In all the millions of heated words the controversy has generated I have heard no explanations – none at all – why a London government is suddenly hell-bent on such a bridge, nor why it should be the only stretch of major road in Scotland not built with Government money, nor why it should cost an arm and a leg to cross it. It is said that the demand comes from the Islanders, but you never find out who has said it, nor how whoever has said it knows that it is the case. Certainly many Islanders loathe the prospect and I loathe it with them. What no-one knows is how many Islanders, because no-one has asked them all. A public inquiry addressed only the style of the bridge, not the infinitely more vexing question of whether or not there should be a bridge at all. The obvious solution of an Island referendum was dismissed for no reason whatsoever, so it seems we will never know whether they want a bridge or not. What we do know is that nature does not.

Nature did away with Skye's land bridge eons ago and has been fashioning an increasingly rarefied Island environment ever since. Nature has linked Skye and the mainland exquisitely with a narrow stretch of sea, and for as long as people have lived on Skye, that has been all the bridge they have ever needed. The fact that today's generations of Islanders experience ferry problems for a few frantic summer months is not sufficient reason to overturn the evolution of the millennia, a piffling and unworthy excuse to create a peninsula out of Skye where nature decreed an island, the one earlier generations christened *The* Island.

Much nature will be obliterated by the bridge, not least the otter strongholds around Kyleakin and Eilean Ban. You can argue, of course, that Skye has many otters, and so it has, but it is surely a fatally flawed argument which permits attacks on one of the few strongholds of a creature which has been systematically purged from old haunts all across the country.

It is ironic too that the bridge has sunk a gruesome midstream anchor on Eilean Ban, for it was there that Gavin Maxwell toiled to establish a wildlife sanctuary in the last years of his life. It was to be a place where people could come and watch wildlife in a wild and stunningly beautiful natural setting. He died before his dream could become a reality. But suppose he had not died, and suppose his dream had been realised, and suppose it had been successful. Imagine the clamour there would have been now at the prospect of this overwhelming despoliation of his island sanctuary, for Maxwell was a supreme publicist for nature and won it countless friends and champions. It is quite possible that the bridge would have been defeated for the sake of Eilean Ban, yet it has never even been seriously contested for the sake of the whole Island of Skye.

A Skye bridge is not a new idea, of course, and one of the more celebrated proponents of a bridge was Alexander Nicolson of Sgurr Alasdair fame. Ben Humble remarks on the fact in *The Cuillin of*

Skye, and bearing in mind its 1952 publication date, adds a pointed period-piece footnote:

(Nicolson) foresaw Skye as a supreme attraction for tourists, and as long ago as 1872 was suggesting that a bridge might easily be built across the narrow stretch of water between Kyle of Lochalsh and Kyleakin. The subject is still appropriate though the ferry is now much more efficient than formerly.

Mercifully, Nicolson's crackpot ideas for three grand hotels at Camasunary and his vision of Skye as the 'Oberland of Scotland' were stillborn, but with the precedent of the bridge established, who knows what other precious sanctities of nature will be breached and discarded?

So why should all this issue forth from a lump on the high moors between Portree and Bracadale? Because from here you *see* the evidence, physical and psychological, of the dilution of Skye's islandness, the faltering of the heartbeat. So much of that which once set Skye apart, the principal guardian of which was its islandness, has been degraded or sold off or obliterated, and never for a good reason. Even the mountain heart is tainted. More important for people, the moorland heart which fed the lifeblood to the Islanders for so long is bruised and battered, raped and smothered. The very language with which Skye named itself, and in which the Islanders fashioned every aspect of their culture, is a rusting lock. It may yet be renovated and freed, what with the Gaelic College of Sal Mor Ostaig on Sleat and the unprecedented exposure of the language on television and in rock and folk music. But a centuries-old thread of continuity is already snapped. That much is already lost.

I look out on this moor, where for so much of the Island's human history, nature and Islander have served each other's cause well, and I see with my own eyes that it has all lurched fatally out of kilter –

fatally for nature, for the Islander's partnership with the Island, possibly even fatally for the very Heart of Skye itself. I watch the march of the gray weather snuffing colour from the moor as it crosses the Island. It might as well be the march of our own shadow hell-bent on draining the moor of its living shades. The anaemic pallor beneath the gray cloud is the shade we have in store for that Skye ever more rigidly shackled and bridged to the mainland. It is caused by the failing of the sources of Island lifeblood.

The Island is the land and the people, and although the population is a third of what it once was and the tourist seasons are not what they were, our capacity to manipulate the landscape has increased beyond the recognition and comprehension of our forefathers, even our fathers. It is a curiously blind human failing that we have used that knowledge only to degrade the land and distance ourselves from it, given that we also have the knowledge to restore it and come closer to it. The Heart of Skye will be a vigorous pulse again only when the Islander learns again what he once knew – how to live closer to the Island.

Chapter Sixteen

There Is No Hurry

HOUSES STAND around the moorland edges of the road, small and mostly white, the staple Skye mix of traditional croft houses and bad bungalows, well spaced and disorderly like curious cattle. In their midst (but some distance away from them), the apparent object of their curiosity, is the telephone box.

All around on every side, lie the autumn moorland miles; beyond in the west, the Minch. The isolation of the phone box reminded me that I had a call to make. Portree's phones had had a small queue of late tourists and rain and I had driven on. Now a few miles up the road there was no queue, nor for that matter any sight or sound of humanity, and the sun and the wind and the softest thistledown rain seemed to seep through the seams of the cloud cloak all over the Island and the Minch. I stopped and phoned, as I talked and listened (the recipient of the call now long forgotten) my attention wavered and wandered out among the hardening Uist hills. Sun splashed on the Minch like thrown coins and I was struck again by the impromptu sorcery of Skye's spells, and the mundanities they transform, such as a telephone box on the edge of a bog. Skye performs such tricks day after day, sometimes many times a day. Time passed and the call lost its point and its seeming importance. Skye has a way of doing that by imposing its own definition of time, which is not a fast one.

I hung up and left the box, niggled at its tenuous connection with worlds beyond the Island, to find that a white-haired woman had been standing patiently behind my back waiting to use the phone, but declining to reveal her presence while I talked. I judged her to be perhaps sixty, sixty-five at a push. She stood bare-headed for all the day's winds and sporadic rains, and with a wind-tanned and almost unlined face that put a splash of serenity about her eyes. She smiled. I apologised. I had not seen her, the call had gone on longer than I had intended, had I known she was there I would have hurried . . . she interrupted all this with a dismissive gesture of head and hand and said:

'There is no hurry. I have all the time in the world.'

When she said 'There is no hurry', she made it sound not so much an expression of her state of mind as an incontrovertible principle of science. There is no oxygen on the moon. There is no hurry.

I had held the door of the phone box open to usher her in. Instead she took it from me and let it close while she stood talking. Was I on holiday? Well yes and no, using a holiday from newspaper work to research a book about Skye (all this was years ago before I slipped the newspaper noose, this conversation all that survived of that wretched effort at a first book), but . . . Oh, a book! Well it was nice to find someone who could do that kind of work and still take time off to chat to an old, done woman. Her voice placed its accents in the manner of a tongue more at ease in Gaelic than English, and within moments (and without seeming to ask a single personal question) she had charmed a brief autobiography out of me.

She found points of contact and common ground in what I told her and the journalist in me began to turn the talk towards her, for apart from being herself for her own sake, she was also my stroke of good fortune, a small insight for me under the surface of the Island through eyes that I could never bring to bear on the place. I think she sensed my enthusiastic interest for what she had to say and her face lit and her eyes shone and she warmed to what it was that was on her mind, and maybe always had been, forever. Skye.

Yes, she was born on Skye, out on Waternish, and eighty-four years ago if you please. I must have registered disbelief in my face, and she doubtless planned it that way. She would know fine she looked the best part of twenty-five years younger. She laughed and said I was not to worry that she had fooled me. She was just lucky – lucky in love for much of her life and lucky to have spent the first twenty years of her life where she did, because it is the first twenty which decide what it is you become. It mattered to her that she had grown up not just where she did but when she did, because that Skye then could keep you going through anything that came after, wherever it happened. Her first twenty years out on Waternish (she made it sound like a different place as well as a different time from what she called 'this Skye now') had borne her through her life. This Skye now, well it was so much harder being young today and she had no wish at all to be young again, not if it meant being young today.

What had brought her back to Skye now? Well, she wasn't what you'd call back, but she'd been coming home to a certain corner of the Island for six weeks every year, her niece's house, as near Waternish as she could get, but not as good, although she did not mind that at all. Just being here and being close was good enough.

Why not as good as Waternish? Well, it was just that there wasn't so much Skye here. Was that 'Skye' she meant or 'sky', I asked? It was Skye, she meant, Skye the Island. Skye in her Waternish-rooted mind meant a tooth of land between two seas. Here (she gestured at the moorland miles) could be anywhere on Skye not Waternish, and so it could, I agreed.

She lived alone now the rest of the year, and she mentioned a small town near Glasgow, a place I knew to have relinquished its old soul years ago to the suffocating cause of Glasgow's commuter belt.

She had gone, she said, like many an Island lass, into domestic service in Glasgow, aged twenty, done well enough at it (although the idea if you think on it as she sometimes did – one person, poor, serving another, not poor, went against the grain even in one as compliant as a Gael . . . she said that matter-of-factly, no bitter hint, not now at least). I thought of that small town under its hillside and remembered it as dark and dull and land-locked, and I grew angry within at the thought of such a shining Island light hidden under such a drab mainland bush.

She'd grown up speaking Gaelic? Yes, oh yes, yes, and it would never be anything other than the Mother Tongue, and she said it as if it should have capital letters. Her face with the sun full on it shaded quite suddenly, and that small transformation let me in a little (an inkling, barely glimpsed and as moving as it was fleeting) on what it was that has left Gaeldom. She could not remember the last time she went a whole day speaking only Gaelic, and if she could remember she would probably weep because it would show how many, many years ago it must have been. Now, who would she talk to? Not her niece, I suggested. No, no, no, not her niece. Was that strange to me, she wondered, strange that she had never lived on Skye for sixty years and more and still she was uneasy in English, yet her niece who had hardly lived a moment anywhere off the Island was so self-conscious about Gaelic?

You know, they tried to knock it out of the children's heads for so long, and until much more recently than I might think. That at least had stopped, and 'they' had done a good job with the state of Gaelic now. But not with her generation. As if anything you took to like your mother's milk could ever be knocked out of you!

She was quiet for a while, and I wanted her back on the subject of what Gaelic had become, because I sensed in that 'they' a certain unease. Surely, I said, it's better now? There's the Gaelic College, evening classes all over Scotland – one I had encountered in as un-

Gaelic a place as Peebles – and the music (the Runrig phenomenon was in its infancy) is reaching a new generation, and Sorley's poetry was before a wider audience than ever now and being taught in schools, and there were many disciples among the new poets. Isn't there a real revival?

Well, it was all very praiseworthy she said, and if it sounded faint praise it was not intended to damn. But it was not the way to save Gaelic, nor was it the way to hear Gaelic. All it meant was that more people were learning the language again, no, not even the language, the words, what they sound like and what they mean. It does not make more Gaels, she said. Folk can use the words but they cannot live the language, and that was the tragedy of Gaelic. It had been too long since the people lived the language. It could only be taught in that way as she was taught it, at her mother's knee.

So did she not speak it at all now? Not often, no. Oh, there had been an old friend in Glasgow she used to meet, an Island woman too, and they used to sit in the corner of some tea room or other and blether away, but even they had begun to be self-conscious about it there, like a pair of performing museum pieces, she said, but at that she laughed and the shading was off her face and she said:

'This might interest you for your book. I sometimes still think in Gaelic, especially when it's something very deep and important to me. And I know I dream in Gaelic, so I always have sweet dreams!' And at that she was laughing again. The sun was out on her face again. She was havering away, she said, and I was to pay no attention to her, me with my work to be doing, and she had to be phoning Archie, but it had been a lovely chat. It had, I said, it most certainly had.

I was halfway back to the car when she called:

'Give us a good book, mind. You'll have to turn a blind eye on some of our faults and play up our saving graces, won't you!'

With that – and I swear she winked – we parted, anonymous

friends. But it was fully ten years ago now, more or less, which would put her in her mid-nineties. I like to think of her still walking to the telephone box and not looking a day over, say, seventy, although it is just as likely that for one reason or another she no longer makes the journey home to form a patient queue of one by the phone. It was another six or seven years before I prised myself free of my old newspaper trade, four more before I made the space and found the publisher for the Skye book which had evolved in my mind for so long. Besides, it is not written in her language and I suspect she may have little enough time for mine. All that I can tell her is that this is a better book than I could ever have written then.

I walked back to the car with the wind in my ears and the Minch in my eyes and her face and the sound of her voice and her graciousness in my mind, and I think I borrowed from her briefly the sadness and the elation of that last withering autumn flourish of her age, which rightly or wrongly sees only a last winter ahead with no prospect of a second spring, for I never felt the same way again, I never knew her name, and I never saw her again.

I have always remembered her expression comparing the bog-edge where we met to Waternish: 'there is not so much Skye here,' she had said. There was more Skye in her than in anyone I ever met. The last of her that I saw she was holding the door of the phone box with one hand and waving with the other, and if I could have that moment in time again I would have asked her to talk all day for me.

But that was then, and it was a different Skye I was seeking then from the one I have come a little closer to since, and I didn't ask her, and for that reason as much as any other I can think of, the Heart of Skye is still that much more elusive than it might otherwise have been.

Selected Bibliography

Barnett, T Ratcliffe – *Autumns in Skye, Ross and Sutherland* (JOHN GRANT, 1946)

Baxter, Colin and Crumley, Jim – *St Kilda* (COLIN BAXTER, 1988)

Craig, David – *On the Crofters' Trail* (JONATHAN CAPE, 1990)

Gordon, Seton – *The Charm of Skye* (CASSELL, 1929) – *Afoot in Wild Places* (CASSELL, 1937)

Humble, Ben – *The Cuillin of Skye* (ERNEST PRESS, 1952, Facsimile edition 1986)

Hunter, James and MacLean, Cailean – *Skye, The Island* (MAINSTREAM 1986)

Maclean, Sorley – *Collected Poems* (CARCANET, 1989)

Maxwell, Gavin – *Ring of Bright Water* (LONGMANS 1960) – *The Rocks Remain* (LONGMANS 1963) – *Raven Seek Thy Brother* (LONGMANS 1968)

Poucher, W A – *The Magic of Skye* (CHAPMAN AND HALL, 1949)

Raine, Kathleen – *Collected Poems* (ALLEN AND UNWIN, 1981) – *The Lion's Mouth* (HAMISH HAMILTON, 1977)

Swire, Otta F – *Skye – The Island and Its Legends* (BLACKIE, 1961)

ST